Modern Critical Interpretations

William Shakespeare's
Henry V

Modern Critical Interpretations

These and other titles in preparation

Modern Critical Interpretations

William Shakespeare's
Henry V

Edited and with an introduction by

Harold Bloom
Sterling Professor of the Humanities
Yale University

Chelsea House Publishers ◊ *1988*

NEW YORK ◊ NEW HAVEN ◊ PHILADELPHIA

© 1988 by Chelsea House Publishers,
a division of Chelsea House Educational Communications, Inc.,
345 Whitney Avenue, New Haven, CT 06511
95 Madison Avenue, New York, NY 10016
5068B West Chester Pike, Edgemont, PA 19028

Introduction © 1988 by Harold Bloom

Printed and bound in the United States of America

10 9 8 7 6 5 4 3 2 1

∞ The paper used in this publication meets the minimum
requirements of the American National Standard for
Permanence of Paper for Printed Library Materials,
Z39.48–1984.

Library of Congress Cataloging-in-Publication Data
William Shakespeare's Henry V.
    (Modern critical interpretations)
    Bibliography: p.
    Includes index.
    1. Shakespeare, William, 1564–1616.   Henry V.
2. Henry V, King of England, 1387–1422, in fiction,
drama, poetry, etc.   I. Bloom, Harold.   II. Series.
PR2812.W55   1988   822.3′3   87–15778
ISBN 0–87754–927–3 (alk. paper)

Contents

Editor's Note

This book gathers together a representative selection of the best modern critical interpretations of Shakespeare's *The Life of Henry the Fifth*. The critical essays are reprinted here in the chronological order of their original publication. I am grateful to John Rogers for his assistance in editing this volume.

My introduction ponders the effect of Falstaff's absence from the play. Anne Barton begins the chronological sequence of criticism with a study of how Shakespeare subverts folk motifs and their previous incorporation into history plays written shortly before his own.

The focus moves to rhetoric in James L. Calderwood's reading of the scenes with Katherine and of other aspects of the use of the English language in *Henry V*. Separate views of the play, as patriotic celebration or ironic vision of a Machiavel masking as Christian monarch, are integrated by Norman Rabkin's demonstration that by apparent design the text works to subvert one view with the other.

David Quint examines Renaissance estimates of Alexander, Caesar, and the ideal Prince, and finds *Henry V* to be a Shakespearean critique of Humanist accounts of history. Something of the same conclusion is implicit in James R. Siemon's analysis of the relation between icons and iconoclasm in the play.

The matrix of history and ideology in *Henry V* is studied by Jonathan Dollimore and Alan Sinfield, with particular reference to the question of the Earl of Essex. Peter Erickson concludes this volume with a comparison between Henry IV and Falstaff as the fathers that Henry V subsumes in his own person, in a strong attempt to escape both his actual father's guilt and his own.

Introduction

The Life of Henry the Fifth does not enjoy much critical esteem in comparison with Shakespeare's other mature histories, but it is a remarkable play if one allows its ironies their full scope. The absence of Falstaff is the largest presence in this drama, since Hal is thereby absent also. Patriotic bombast abounds, and even a touch of Falstaff (or Hal) would destroy that rhetoric of gorgeous deception essential to the celebration of English prowess against the overdressed French. If we shipped Falstaff from Shrewsbury to Agincourt and the fat knight went into the battle there, carrying a bottle of sack instead of a pistol in his case or holster, would not the play break apart? *Henry the Fifth* can scarcely sustain its few overt references to Falstaff and dares not bring him on stage even to die before us. "The King has kill'd his heart," says Mistress Quickly, and the otherwise hyperbolical Pistol adds, in all truth: "His heart is fracted and corroborate." I do not read that last word as an error for "corrupted," but as a sad indication that Falstaff so loves Hal that he has agreed to his own rejection and so wills to die.

Nothing else in *Henry the Fifth* touches the sublimity and pathos of Mistress Quickly and Falstaff's followers recounting his final moments:

> BARD: Would I were with him, wheresome'er he is, either
>   in heaven or in hell!
> HOST: Nay sure, he's not in hell; he's in Arthur's bosom,
>   if ever man went to Arthur's bosom. 'A made a
>   finer end, and went away and it had been any
>   christom child. 'A parted ev'n just between twelve
>   and one, ev'n at the turning o' th' tide; for after I
>   saw him fumble with the sheets, and play with

1

flowers, and smile upon his finger's end, I knew
there was but one way; for his nose was as sharp as
a pen, and 'a [babbl'd] of green fields. "How now,
Sir John?" quoth I, "what, man? be a' good cheer."
So 'a cried out, "God, God, God!" three or four
times. Now I, to comfort him, bid him 'a should
not think of God; I hop'd there was no need to
trouble himself with any such thoughts yet. So 'a
bade me lay more clothes on his feet. I put my
hand into the bed and felt them, and they were as
cold as any stone; then I felt to his knees, and so
up'ard and up'ard, and all was as cold as any stone.

NYM: They say he cried out of sack.

HOST: Ay, that 'a did.

BARD: And of women.

HOST: Nay, that 'a did not.

BOY: Yes, that 'a did, and said they were dev'ls incarnate.

HOST: 'A could never abide carnation—'twas a color he
never lik'd.

BOY: 'A said once, the dev'l would have him about
women.

HOST: 'A did in some sort, indeed, handle women; but
then he was rheumatic, and talk'd of the whore of
Babylon.

BOY: Do you not remember, 'a saw a flea stick upon
Bardolph's nose, and 'a said it was a black soul
burning in hell?

BARD: Well, the fuel is gone that maintain'd that fire.
That's all the riches I got in his service.

(2.3.7–44)

This is a broken Falstaff, facing the four last things of death,
judgment, heaven, and hell, not as Dives, the purple-clad glutton of
Luke 16:22ff., but as a beggar and a child, playing with flowers,
smiling in a second innocence, and poignantly crying out against
sack and women—but in vain, for who can envision Sir John Falstaff
without a wench and a bottle? The boy reminds us of the knight's
preternatural wit and its butt, Bardolph, reminds us of his master's
hand-to-mouth economy of existence. Does Mistress Quickly's

"rheumatic" mean "lunatic," and does the greatest of wits die as his true descendant Oscar Wilde died, as a repentent sinner, near madness? I think not. Rather, Shakespeare gives us an outrageous Falstaff, who dies as he has lived, but in a finer tone, his bed crowded with apocalyptic visions, not of Doll Tearsheet, but of the Whore of Babylon. She is the emblem of royal power, of every earthly tyranny however popular, and so a version of the goddess of war. That Falstaff, ironic subverter of royal pomp and power, should die discoursing about her is a very oblique but highly apposite commentary upon the royal crusade of Henry V against France.

If that seems excessive, since Henry V manifestly is a patriotic hero, precursor to the great Elizabeth, then consider the king's threats to Harfleur, complete with "naked infants spitted upon pikes," and his fairly consistent record of systematic brutality, including a shrugging-off that sends poor Bardolph, an old crony, to execution. No, Shakespeare knew better what he did than we tend to acknowledge, and his portrait of Henry V is both ironic and celebratory, but not in a balance. If you are Rudyard Kipling, then Henry V is a demigod of war, victory, splendor, and British superiority, but if you are William Hazlitt, then the great warrior is "a very amiable monster." He is an exemplary Christian king, hard and shrewd, who murders prisoners without remorse and seems to see through everything and everyone, himself presumably included. But that returns us to one of Shakespeare's greatest powers, the representation of change in the psyche. Long after he has rejected his teacher Falstaff, Hal benefits from the great ironist's lesson, which is to keep your freedom by seeing through every idea of order or code of moral behavior. Poor Falstaff was right to babble of the Whore of Babylon, because his pupil ends as a more efficient Bolingbroke, free of his father's guilt—a new and greater Fortinbras rather than another Hamlet.

Still, if we can see the Earl of Essex in the character of Fortinbras or Henry V, though not in Hamlet, then the hero of Shakespeare's play might as well have been Essex had not Essex come to a very bad end. Hamlet and Falstaff are counter-Machiavels, but Henry V is the perfect prince as sketched by Machiavelli. So large and profound are Shakespeare's ironies that Henry V in the context of his own play could not be bettered as a hero. His play is anything but a critique of the hero. The world without Falstaff is not a world without imagination, but its largest being, Henry V, is only as large as life. Henry

V is not how meaning gets started. He does not overflow, has no excess of vitality that can give more life to others. But he knows always exactly what he says and what he does, as he knew exactly what he was doing when he banished Falstaff, and Prince Hal with him.

As in the much greater *Antony and Cleopatra,* Shakespeare lets you read yourself in him without seeking to alter you, whoever you are. If you are a reductionist, then Antony is in his dotage and Cleopatra is and will be always what she was, an imperial strumpet. If you yield to imagination, then Antony is a more generous Hercules, and Cleopatra a prophetess of the Sublime, who fuses herself into her own immortal longings. So is it in *Henry the Fifth;* the reductionist gets the ideal warrior-king, while the person who knows that the imagination wishes to be indulged ends with a nostalgia for the young man who sojourned in the taverns and on the highways with Falstaff. That sojourn was itself Machiavellian, a counterfeiting that taught excellence in counterfeiting, but the playgoer or reader learns what Henry V could not afford to know, which is that "to die is to be a counterfeit . . . but to counterfeit dying, when a man thereby liveth, is to be no counterfeit, but the true and perfect image of life indeed," which is to be Falstaff.

The King Disguised:
The Two Bodies of Henry V

Anne Barton

In the worst moment of the French campaign, when the night before Agincourt finds the English army reduced, dispirited, and ailing, "even as men wrack'd upon a sand, that look to be wash'd off the next tide" (4.1.97–98), Henry V pays two quite different visits to his despondent troops. Although the first of them, made in his own person as king, is not enacted, the Chorus testifies eloquently to its success:

> every wretch, pining and pale before,
> Beholding him, plucks comfort from his looks.
> A largess universal like the sun
> His liberal eye doth give to every one,
> Thawing cold fear, that mean and gentle all,
> Behold, as may unworthiness define,
> A little touch of Harry in the night.
>
> (4.41–47)

Later, in the first scene of act 4, Henry borrows a cloak from Sir Thomas Erpingham, conceals his royal identity, and ventures alone among soldiers no longer able to recognize him as their king. His fortunes in this second sally are altogether less prosperous. Thorny and disquieting from the start, his conversation with Williams, Court, and Bates ends in an open quarrel. Moreover, it provokes Henry's

From *The Triple Bond: Plays, Mainly Shakespearean, in Performance,* edited by Joseph G. Price. © 1975 by Pennsylvania State University. Pennsylvania State University Press, 1975.

only soliloquy in the play: a bitter examination of kingship itself and of the irremovable barriers isolating the monarch from a world of private men.

Shakespeare may well have remembered from Holinshed, or from *The First English Life of Henry V,* that the historical Henry "daylie and nightlie in his owne person visited the watches, orders and stacions of everie part of his hoast." Nowhere, however, is it suggested that he ever did so incognito. Geoffrey Bullough has argued that when Shakespeare made Henry muffle himself in Erpingham's cloak he was thinking of a passage from Tacitus's *Annals* in which Germanicus disguises himself on the eve of a battle in order to assess the morale of the Roman legions. Germanicus, however, lurks outside his soldiers' tents as a mere eavesdropper; he never attempts a personal encounter. Although the passage cannot be discounted entirely as a source for Henry's disguise, its importance has surely been overestimated. For those Elizabethans who watched *Henry V* in the new Globe theatre in 1599, the king's behavior before Agincourt would have had analogues far more striking and immediate. There is a surprising number of disguised kings to be found in those English history plays which have survived from the period 1587–1600. A few of these princes are driven to dissemble their identity for a time out of political necessity, as Marlowe's Edward II does after the triumph of Young Mortimer and Queen Isabella, or Shakespeare's Henry VI in the last part of the trilogy, when he rashly steals across the border into England "disguised, with a prayerbook," only to be recognized despite this precaution by the two Keepers and haled away to the Tower. A larger and more interesting group is composed of kings who, like Shakespeare's Henry V, adopt disguise as a caprice, for reasons that are fundamentally exploratory and quixotic.

Toward the end of *George a Greene, the Pinner of Wakefield* (?Robert Greene, ca. 1590), an unspecified King Edward of England decides to "make a merrie journey for a moneth" along with his friend King James of Scotland, for the purpose of meeting the folk hero George a Greene, a loyal pinner in the north country who has been instrumental in putting down a rebellion against the Crown. The two monarchs travel on foot and in disguise. At the town of Bradford they yield meekly to the insolent demands of the locals, trailing their staves in order to pass without argument through the town. George a Greene, disgusted by such pusillanimity, berates the two kings soundly for cowardice and forces them to hold up their staves. King Edward gains a vivid and somewhat disconcerting idea of the character and temper of his subject before the revelation of his royal identity puts an end to the game. All is forgiven. George is offered a knighthood, which he politely refuses, preferring to remain an English yeoman. Edward unites him with Bettris, his love, overriding the snobbish objections of her father, and the play ends harmoniously with a feast at which King Edward, King James, George a Greene, Robin Hood and Maid Marian, and all the shoemakers of Bradford sit side by side as friends and good companions.

Peele's *Edward I* (ca. 1591) also associates the king in disguise with the Robin Hood stories. Lluellen, the rebellious prince of Wales, his mistress Elinor, and his friend Rice ap Meredith have taken to the greenwood in the company of a friar, "to live and die together like Chamber-Britaines, Robin Hood, Little John, Frier Tucke, and Maide Marrian." King Edward, intrigued to learn of this little society, decides to pay it a secret visit, disguised, and accompanied only by Lluellen's brother, Sir David of Brecknock:

> as I am a Gentleman,
> Ile have one merrie flirt with little John,
> And Robin Hood, and his Maide Marian.
> Be thou my counsell and my companie,
> And thou maist Englands resolution see.
> (10.1548–52)

In the forest, Edward adjudicates in a dispute between two rogues who have tried to cozen one another, agrees with Lluellen that his purse will belong to whichever man can overcome the other in a fair fight, and (exactly as his prototype Richard Coeur de Lion had done in the ballads) sends "Robin Hood" sprawling. The exigencies of Peele's plot made it impossible for this forest scene to end with reconciliation and pardon in the ballad tradition. Lluellen, rebellious to the end, is killed in battle later in the play. It is remarkable, however, how close this personal encounter between the outlaw and the king he cannot recognize—in both senses of the word—has come to healing the breach between them. When "Longshanks" has gone, his identity disclosed, Lluellen admits ruefully that "his courage is like to the Lion, and were it not that rule and soveraigntie set us at jarre, I could love and honour the man for his valour" (12.1917–19).

The two anonymous plays *Fair Em* (ca. 1590) and *The True*

Chronicle History of King Leir (ca. 1590) both present kings who disguise themselves in the cause of love. William the Conqueror, in *Fair Em,* falls in love with a picture of Blanch, Princess of Denmark, and travels to see her in her father's court under the name of Sir Robert of Windsor. Finding the lady less glamorous in reality than she seemed in her portrait, he tries to elope with Mariana, a lady promised to his friend and traveling companion, the Marquis of Lubeck. Mariana, however, not only surmounts the temptation to abandon Lubeck for a crown but contrives to substitute a masked and lovesick Blanch for herself at the rendezvous appointed. William, who discovers the fraud on arrival in England, is understandably put out but decides that although Blanch is not Mariana she is nonetheless tolerable, and certainly preferable to war with Denmark. At the end of the play, William marries Blanch and, at the same time, restores Godard the supposed miller to his rightful place in society and bestows his daughter Em upon Valingford, the suitor who best deserves her.

In *King Leir,* the Gallian king comes to England disguised as a pilgrim, in order to determine which is the best and most marriageable of Leir's three daughters. He meets Cordella after her disgrace, finds her fair and good, and pretends that he has been sent as an ambassador by his royal master to make her the Gallian queen. Cordella, who has most perspicaciously fallen in love with the humble palmer himself, spurns this splendid offer and bids him "cease for thy King, seeke for thy selfe to woo." After this gratifying proof that Cordella loves the man and not the monarch, the palmer reveals his identity and the two are married immediately and return to France. Disguise, however, remains a feature of their court. In scene 24, the Gallian king and queen mingle with their subjects in the guise of country folk and, thus obscured, discover and are reconciled with the wretched Leir and his counsellor Perillus on the seacoast of Brittany.

Finally, *The First Part of King Edward IV,* a play written by Thomas Heywood before 1599, presents two quite separate royal disguises. Edward conceals his identity when he goes into Lombard Street for the first time to lay amorous siege to Mistress Shore. More relevant to *Henry V,* however, is his encounter with John Hobs the tanner. The king, hunting incognito at Drayton Basset, becomes separated from his queen and courtiers. Hobs, meeting him in the forest, suspects him at first for a thief ("How these roysters swarm in the country, now the King is so near"), but is persuaded at length that Edward is a minor hanger-on at court: in fact, the king's butler. Under this delusion, he prattles on merrily about the two kings of England, Edward at court and the deposed Henry VI in the Tower. Edward, slyly anxious to know how he is regarded by this outspoken subject, receives some disconcertingly frank answers to the questions he puts. The commons of England, according to Hobs, love King Edward

> as poor folk love holidays, glad to have them now and then; but to have them come too often will undo them. So, to see the King now and then 'tis comfort; but every day would beggar us; and I may say to thee, we fear we shall be troubled to lend him money; for we doubt he's but needy.

Even more improbable in its light-hearted political inconsequence is Edward's amused acceptance of the tanner's shifting loyalties. "Shall I say my conscience?" he inquires cunningly. "I think Harry is the true king."

> HOBS: Art advised of that? Harry's of the old house of
>   Lancaster; and that progeny do I love.
> KING: And thou dost not hate the house of York?
> HOBS: Why, no; for I am just akin to Sutton Windmill; I
>   can grind which way soe'er the wind blow. If it be
>   Harry, I can say, "Well fare, Lancaster." If it be
>   Edward, I can sing, "York, York, for my money."

Basically, as it turns out, Hobs approves of King Edward for reasons that have nothing to do with his government of the realm: "He's a frank franion, a merry companion, and loves a wench well." To his way of thinking, the king ought not to encourage patents and monopolies, but Hobs is willing to believe that Edward does so out of ignorance, because he has been misled by greedy counsellors and because he cannot see for himself how the system operates. As subject and king converse, Edward's respect for this "honest true tanner" and for his powers of observation grows. Hobs, for his part, comes to like the supposed butler so well that he invites him home to his cottage for dinner and the night. The tanner has a pretty daughter and there is even some talk of a match, although Hobs would like his prospective son-in-law to have a steadier profession, not one of these fly-by-night court posts. Not until daybreak does

Edward tear himself away from the tanner's hospitality to return to London and the troubles of a kingdom in revolt. Again, the meeting between subject and king in disguise has generated harmony, good fellowship, and mutual understanding.

In all these English histories—and there must have been many more plays like them, now lost—the king's disguise demands to be seen as a romantic gesture. Edward IV, William the Conqueror, Edward I, the Gallian king, or the brace of monarchs in *George a Greene,* all conceal their identities in much the spirit of Haroun al Raschid, the caliph of *The Arabian Nights* who liked to walk the streets of Baghdad incognito, in search of the marvellous and the strange. Moreover, the people they meet come from the world of balladry and legend. Robin Hood and Maid Marian, the folk-hero George a Greene, the miller and his daughter, thieves and outlaws, the beggar-maid destined to become a queen, or the tanner of Tamworth: all were characters nurtured in the popular imagination. Maurice Keen, in *The Outlaws of Medieval Legend,* describes the informal meeting of commoner and king as the wish-dream of a peasantry harried and perplexed by a new class of officials, an impersonal bureaucracy against which the ordinary man seemed to have no redress:

> They only knew that the King was the ultimate repository of a law whose justice they acknowledged, and they saw treason against him as a betrayal of their allegiance to God himself. If they could only get past his corrupt officers, whose abuse of the trust reposed in them amounted to treason in itself, and bring their case before the King, they believed that right would be done. Their unshakeable faith in the King's own justice was the most tragic of the misconceptions of the medieval peasantry, and the balladmakers and their audiences shared it to the full.

In the ballads, king and unsuspecting subject meet time after time and discover unanimity of opinion and mutual respect. Richard Coeur de Lion banquets in Sherwood Forest on stolen venison, forgives Robin Hood and his men, and confounds the sheriff of Nottingham. Henry II so enjoys the rough but generous hospitality of the miller of Mansfield that he makes him a knight and gives him a royal license to keep the forest of Sherwood. Other ballads describe the meeting of Edward I and the reeve, King Alfred and the shepherd, Edward IV and the tanner, Henry VIII and the cobbler, James I and the tinker, William III and the forester, and many similar encounters.

That conversations of this sort represent a fantasy, the "misconception," as Keen terms it, of a victimized agrarian class, is obvious. They derive from attitudes far removed from anything which the hardheaded citizens of Elizabeth's London actually believed. Yet the old roots ran deep. This type of ballad not only survived through Jacobean and Caroline times: the idea behind it remained oddly resonant and haunting. Real Tudor monarchs sometimes played at enacting it. Henry VIII, as Hall tells us, graciously allowed himself to be "waylaid" and dragged off to a reconstruction of Coeur de Lion's feast with Robin Hood, Maid Marian, and their fellows. Queen Elizabeth, walking in Wanstead gardens, suddenly found herself confronting a group of supposed country folk: "Though they knew not her estate, yet something there was which made them startle aside and gaze upon her." Cunningly, Philip Sidney proceeded to involve the queen in a dispute between a shepherd and a forester for possession of the Lady of May, requesting her, after she had heard the rustic arguments of both sides, to award the lady to the suitor she considered most deserving. Traces of this kind of situation can be seen as well in some of the masques at court, but it was in the drama proper that the idea of the king's personal engagement with his subjects and their problems flowered and was most fully exploited.

There are a few Elizabethan plays in which the king manages to mingle with his subjects freely and dispense justice without resorting to disguise. At the end of Dekker's *The Shoemaker's Holiday*, Henry V in his own person sweeps away the snobbery of his officers and nobles:

> Dost thou not know that love respects no blood,
> Cares not for difference of birth or state?
> The maid is young, well born, fair, virtuous,
> A worthy bride for any gentleman.

As benevolent *deus ex machina*, he joins the hands of Rose, the citizen's daughter, and Lacy, nephew to the earl of Lincoln. Annihilating objections based upon wealth or class, he acts from principles of perfect equity as soon as he examines the case himself, just as the medieval minstels had always believed he would. Yet even Dekker's Henry, in a play which could scarcely be described as realistic, worries about the constraints and inhibitions which his declared royal presence may impose on London's madcap mayor, Simon Eyre, at the Shrove Tuesday banquet where these events take place. Most Elizabethan dramatists seem to have accepted the idea that disguise was an essential prerequisite for the ease and success of the meeting between private man and king. Only if the king's identity was concealed could there be natural conversation, frankness, and a sense of rapport. It is the fundamental premise of all these plays that the king, rightly considered, is but a man, and a remarkably understanding man at that. If only, they seem to suggest, king and commoner could talk together in this way, without formality or embarrassment, how many problems would be solved, how many popular grievances redressed. Humanity and humor, an easy cameraderie: these qualities, usually obscured by ceremony, distance, and that hierarchy of officials standing between the monarch and his people, emerge clearly as soon as he steps down from his throne to speak, for a little while, as a private man.

When Shakespeare sent Henry V to converse incognito with Williams, Court, and Bates on the night before Agincourt, he was surely influenced by plays like these far more than by any distant memory of how Germanicus had behaved in the war against Arminius. Generically, Shakespeare's disguised king belongs with Peele's Edward I, Heywood's Edward IV, or the accommodating monarchs of *George a Greene*. Yet the *Henry V* episode is unique. By 1599, the king who freely chooses disguise had become the hallmark of a particular kind of play. Polonius almost certainly would have defined the mode (quite shrewdly) as the "comical-historical." *Henry V*, however, is not a comical history. Far more ironic and complicated than the plays which belong properly to that genre, it introduces the timeworn and popular dramatic motif of the king disguised into its fourth act in order to question, not to celebrate, a folk convention. In itself, the gesture could be relied upon to generate certain clearly defined emotional expectations in an Elizabethan audience powerfully conditioned by both a ballad and a stage tradition. Shakespeare built upon this fact. He used Henry's disguise to summon up the memory of a wistful, naive attitude toward history and the relationship of subject and king which this play rejects as attractive but untrue: a nostalgic but false romanticism.

As the royal captain of a ruined band, a sun-god radiating his beams indiscriminately upon the soldiers among whom he walks, Henry is effective, as the Chorus makes plain. Throughout this play, the relation between the Chorus's unequivocal celebration of Henry and his war in France and the complicated, ambiguous, and sometimes flatly contradictory scenes which these speeches are made to introduce is productive of irony and double focus. This duality of attitude is particularly striking in act IV, where the Chorus's epic account of the king dispensing comfort to his troops in his own person leads directly into that altogether more dubious scene in which Henry visits the army a second time, disguised, in the manner of a ballad king. Once he has obliterated his identity, Henry falls into a series of nonencounters, meetings in which the difficulty of establishing understanding between subject and king is stressed, not the encouraging effect of "a little touch of Harry in the night" (4.47).

It is true that Ancient Pistol, the first man Henry faces, is scarcely capable of rational discourse. Pistol lives in a wholly private world, a heightened and extravagant realm where everything appears twice life size. His overcharged style of speech, filled with contempt for Fortune, exotic geography, and resounding proper names, derives from Marlowe and from those lesser dramatists who imitated Marlowe. Pistol's language is a tissue of play scraps. In his own mind, as Leslie Hotson has pointed out, he is Tamburlaine. "As good a gentleman as the emperor" (4.1.42), he appears blatantly literary, a mere stage king, as soon as he confronts Henry. Linguistically, Shakespeare's early histories had been intermittently Marlovian. Here, at the end of his Elizabethan cycle, he effectively laid the ghost of Tamburlaine as a hero, making it impossible for him to be taken seriously again until the Restoration. By deliberately weighing Pistol's egotism, his histrionics, against the workaday prose of the true king, he indicated the distance between one kind of theatrical fantasy and fact.

Perhaps because he fears recognition by his captains, Henry makes no attempt to speak to Fluellen and Gower. He waits in silence until the entry of Williams, Court, and Bates: three ordinary soldiers for whom the king has always been an unapproachable and distant figure. This encounter is, of course, the mirror image of all those scenes in plays like *George a Greene* or *Edward IV* in which the king and his humble subject reach a frank and mutual accord. Here, nothing of the kind occurs. Instead, Henry finds himself embroiled in a tough and increasingly embarrassing argument. He is rhetorically dexterous, and he succeeds in convincing the soldiers that the king cannot be held responsible for the particular state of soul of those individuals who die in his wars. The other question raised by Williams, that of the goodness of the king's cause in itself, his heavy reckoning at that latter day when he must confront the subjects who have been mutilated and have died for him in a war that perhaps was unjust, Henry simply evades. Here, as in the play as a whole, it is left standing, unresolved.

Even worse, Henry discovers with a sense of shock that his soothing account of the king as "but a man, as I am" (4.1.101–2), sensitive to the disapprobation or approval of his humblest subject, is treated as flatly absurd. For Williams, the gulf between commoner and king is unbridgeable. A man "may as well go about to turn the sun to ice with fanning in his face with a peacock's feather" as expect his "poor and private displeasure" to influence the behavior of a monarch (4.1.194–99). This shaft strikes home, exposing the speciousness of Henry's pretense that he can really be the friend and brother of these soldiers, as well as their king. The conversation ends in a quarrel, a failure to arrive at understanding which contradicts the romantic, ballad tradition. Left alone, Henry meditates acrimoniously on the pains of sovereignty, the doubtful worth of the "ceremony" that divides the king from a world of private men without providing him with any adequate compensation for his isolation and his crippling weight of responsibility.

Subsequently, after Agincourt has been won, Williams learns that it was the king himself whom he offended and with whom he has promised to fight. Like the outlaws of medieval legend, Williams meets not only with pardon but with royal largesse. He receives his glove again filled with golden crowns by Henry's bounty. Yet this gift, unlike its archetypes in the ballads and in Elizabethan comical histories, seems strangely irrelevant. Consciously anachronistic, it provides not the ghost of an answer to the questions raised during this particular encounter between common man and king disguised. Is the king's cause just? If not, what measure of guilt does he incur for requiring men to die for anything but the strict necessity of their country? Can the opinions and judgments of private men influence the sovereign on his throne? Henry is generous to Williams, but it is a dismissive generosity which places the subject firmly in an inferior position and silences his voice. The two men do not sit down at table together to any common feast, in the manner of Dekker's Henry V or Heywood's Edward IV. Indeed, Williams himself seems to be aware that the answer represented by the glove full of crowns is inadequate. He never thanks Henry for the present, accepting it without a word and turning, in the next instant, to repudiate the shilling offered him by Fluellen: "I will none of your money" (4.8.70). That gift he can dare to refuse. Even his plea for pardon is filled with suppressed anger and resentment:

> Your majesty came not like yourself: you appeared to me but as a common man; witness the night, your garments, your lowliness; and what your highness suffered under that shape, I beseech you, take it for your own fault, and not mine.
>
> (4.8.51–56)

Henry V is a play concerned to force upon its audience a creative participation far more active than usual. The Chorus urges an unceasing visualization, bright pictures in the mind, of horses, ships under sail, silken banners, or the engines of siege warfare. Within the play itself, Shakespeare suggests with indicating priority a multiplicity of possible responses to every character and event. Celebration and denigration, heroism and irony exist uneasily side by side. The Chorus may regard England's despoliation of France as a species of sacred obligation. Elsewhere, the attitude is far less clearcut. Always in the background there hovers a disconcerting memory of Canterbury and Ely in the opening scene, busily fomenting the war in France to divert attention from the temporal wealth of the Church. Behind that lurks Henry IV's deathbed advice to his son to "busy giddy minds with foreign quarrels" (*2 Henry IV,* 4.5.213–14) in the hope that the shaky legitimacy of Lancastrian rule might thus escape scrutiny. Among Shakespeare's other histories, only *Henry VIII* is so deliberately ambiguous, so overtly a puzzle in which the audience is left to forge its own interpretation of action and characters with only minimal guidance from a dramatist apparently determined to stress the equivalence of mutually exclusive views of a particular complex of historical event.

In both *Henry V* and *Henry VIII,* the fact that the mind and heart of the king are essentially opaque, that his true thoughts and feelings remain veiled behind a series of royal poses—as those of Richard II, Richard III, King John, Henry VI, or even Henry IV do not—contributes to the difficulty of assessment. Even Henry's soliloquy before Agincourt is strangely externalized and formal, in no sense a revelation of the private workings of a mind. Neither here nor anywhere else in the play is the whole truth about the king's personal decision to invade France disclosed. This reticence is not accidental. Henry is, by secular standards, an extraordinarily successful example of the God-man incarnate. The conception of kingship in this play derives not from the relaxed and essentially personal tradition of the ballads but from a complicated, inherently tragic Tudor doctrine of the king's two bodies. Shakespeare had previously dealt with the violence of divorce or incompatibility between the twin natures of the king. Henry V, by contrast, has achieved a union of body natural and body politic difficult to flaw. Yet the price he pays for his subordination of the individual to the office is heavy, in personal terms. There is loss as well as gain in the gulf that now divides Henry from his old associates Bardolph and Pistol, from a world of private men in which he alone speaks out of a double nature. Hal's sudden unavailability as a person, his retreat into an oddly declamatory series of stances, reflects neither his own nor Shakespeare's weakness. It is simply a measure of the signal effectiveness of this man's incarnation as king.

In many respects *Henry V* is a success story. Agincourt, at least from one angle, is a splendor. Within its own limited sphere the rhetoric of the Chorus rings true. Henry himself can be described as an "ideal" sovereign, God's gift to an England weary of rebellion, usurpation, and civil war. At the same time, it is not easy for any mere mortal to support the psychological and moral burden of a double self. At a number of points in the play, particularly in situations which seem to demand an essentially personal response, the strain involved in maintaining such a constant ventriloquism becomes obvious. Even when Henry tries temporarily to obliterate one half of his identity, as he does in the scene with Williams, Court, and Bates, he finds it impossible to produce a natural and unforced imitation of a private man. Richard II, ironically enough, had experienced similar difficulties after his deposition. In Henry's case, the suppression of one side of his nature is only momentary, the product of whim rather than political defeat. Nevertheless, his awkwardness with the soldiers points to the irrevocability of that mystic marriage of king and man accomplished in the ceremony of coronation. Only death can dissolve this union.

Meanwhile, the king must contrive to deal with a world of single-natured individuals from which he himself stands conspicuously apart. Henry cannot have personal friends as other men do.

There is a sense in which the rejection of Falstaff at the end of *2 Henry IV* leads directly on to the rejection of the traitor Scroop in the second act of *Henry V*. Precisely because Scroop is someone Henry has imagined was bound to him as a man by private ties of affection and liking, his treason is far more painful than the more neutral betrayal of Cambridge and Grey. With the latter he deals in an efficient, almost perfunctory fashion. Only Scroop evokes a long and suddenly emotional remonstrance in which Henry effectively bids farewell to the possibility of personal relationship. Significantly, this scene at Southampton is placed between the two episodes in London dealing with the death of Falstaff. The epic voyage to France is thus preceded by three scenes dealing not merely with the death of former friends but with the final severance of the new king's remaining personal ties. Thereafter in the play, he will use the term "friend" in a special sense.

Not by accident, Henry abruptly abandons the royal "we" when he turns to accuse Scroop. In act 1 he had spoken almost entirely from this corporate position, allowing himself only infrequently to be jolted into an adventurer's "I." The Southampton scene is also one which insists throughout upon the double nature of the king and makes that nature grammatically clear through his habitual use of a plural first person. Cambridge and Grey, it seems, have conspired to kill "us" (2.2.85–91): "But O, / What shall *I* say to thee, Lord Scroop?" (2.2.93–94). In his long, passionate speech to this false friend "that knew'st the very bottom of my soul" (2.2.97), Henry grieves more as man than as king. Not until the moment comes for sentencing all three conspirators does he regain his balance, discriminating calmly between the offense intended to his body natural and his body politic:

> Touching our person seek we no revenge;
> But we our kingdom's safety must so tender,
> Whose ruin you have sought, that to her laws
> We do deliver you. Get you therefore hence,
> Poor miserable wretches, to your death.
> (2.2.174–78)

The voice here is impersonal, speaking from behind the mask of kingship, deliberately avoiding the first person singular of individual response.

Once arrived in France, Henry refers to himself far more often as "I" or "me" than he does as "we" or "us," at least up to the council of Troyes in the fifth act. As leader of an English host stranded in a foreign country and in a position of increasing danger, Henry finds it not only possible but necessary to simplify his royalty to some extent. After much painful marching in the rain-drenched field, he can describe himself as a soldier, "a name that in my thoughts becomes me best" (3.3.5–6). In this role he achieves a measure of escape from the royal impersonality demanded under more ordinary and formal circumstances. When he warns the governor of Harfleur of the horrors that lie in store for his city if it fails to capitulate, when he exchanges badinage with Fluellen, or celebrates honor in the Crispin day speech in terms that Hotspur would have understood, he is playing a part—much as Prince Hal had done in the tavern scenes of the *Henry IV* plays or among the alien but imitable chivalries of Shrewsbury. In this context, the infrequent appearances of the royal "we" acts 3 and 4 become purposeful and striking reminders of the ineluctable reality of the king's twin nature—a nature temporarily obscured by the adventurer's pose appropriate to the French campaign.

Gravely, Henry reminds Williams that "it was ourself thou didst abuse," before he dismisses him with pardon and reward (4.8.48). When his old associate Bardolph is summarily executed for robbing a church, Fluellen informs the king and, describing the dead man's face in terms so vivid that there can be no possible mistake, inquires somewhat tactlessly: "If your majesty knows the man" (3.6.96–101). Henry's stiff reply to this appeal to his memory of a time before his coronation is more than a politic evasion: "We would have all such offenders so cut off." His sudden use here of the first person plural of majesty, occurring as it does in a scene where even the French herald Montjoy is addressed by Henry as "I," constitutes the real answer to Fluellen's question. As a twin-natured being, the king is stripped not only of personal friends but also of a private past. To recognize Bardolph, let alone to regret him, is impossible.

The war in France provides Henry with "friends" of a rhetorical and special kind. It also allows him an ambiguous use of the pronoun "we" which momentarily clothes the abstract doctrine of the king's two bodies with flesh. Before Harfleur, Henry rallies "dear friends" to the breach, or urges them "to close the wall up with our English dead" (3.1.1–2). The good yeomen whose limbs were made in England are asked to "show us here the mettle of your pasture"

(3.1.26–27). Later, before Agincourt, he will tell his cousin Westmoreland that "if we are mark'd to die, we are enow / To do our country loss" and speak of "we few, we happy few, we band of brothers" (4.3.20–21, 60). His encounter with Williams, Court, and Bates in act 4 is prefaced by a speech addressed to Bedford and Gloucester in which the pronouns "we" and "our" are by implication both royal and collective:

> Gloucester, 'tis true that we are in great danger;
> The greater therefore should our courage be.
> Good morrow, brother Bedford. God Almighty!
> There is some soul of goodness in things evil,
> Would men observingly distil it out;
> For our bad neighbour makes us early stirrers,
> Which is both healthful and good husbandry:
> Besides, they are our outward consciences,
> And preachers to us all; admonishing
> That we should dress us fairly for our end.
> Thus may we gather honey from the weed,
> And make a moral of the devil himself.
>
> (4.1.1–12)

In passages like these, where Henry's "we" and "our" seem to refer both to himself as king and to the nobles and soldiers around him as a group, a community in which he participates, the idea of the king's two bodies acquires a meaning that is concrete and emotionally resonant. Rightly considered, Henry's soldiers are part of his body politic and thus extensions of his own identity. But it is only in moments of stress and mutual dependence that the doctrine articulates itself naturally, allowing the king an easy jocularity which is familiar without being intimate, essentially distant at the same time that it creates an illusion of warmth and spontaneity. As the peril of the situation in France grows, so does Henry's sense of fellowship. It is almost as though he extracts from danger a kind of substitute for the genuinely personal relationships abandoned with Falstaff and Scroop.

Ironically, Henry's dazzling victory at Agincourt necessarily spells the end of this special accord. The king who speaks in the council chamber at Troyes in act 5 is once again firmly entrenched behind a royal "we" that is a diagram rather than a three-dimensional fact. Somewhat disconcertingly, he insists upon using the first-person plural even in his request that the girl he intends to marry should remain in the room with him when the peers of France and England depart to discuss terms of peace:

> Yet leave our cousin Katharine here with us:
> She is our capital demand, compris'd
> Within the fore-rank of our articles.
> (5.2.95–97)

For all its political realism, this seems a desperately awkward beginning to a declaration of love. In the wooing scene that follows, Henry falls back upon his soldier's persona. He resurrects this "I" to deal with a situation of peculiar difficulty. How should a king, encumbered by twin natures, embark upon what is necessarily the most personal of all relationships, that of love? Henry's particular compromise is witty, and yet the problems of communication in this scene do not spring entirely from the fact that the king's French is even more rudimentary than the lady's English. Most of Henry's blunders, his various solecisms, derive from his uncertainty as to whether at a given instant he is speaking as Harry or as England, and whether the girl he addresses is the delectable Kate or the kingdom of France. Certainly the princess, when informed that her suitor loves France so well that "I will not part with a village of it; I will have it all mine: and Kate, when France is mine and I am yours, then yours is France and you are mine," might well be excused for complaining that "I cannot tell wat is dat," even if her linguistic skills were considerably greater than they are (5.2.178–83). The loving monarchs of *Fair Em* and *King Leir* recognized no such problems of expression. Whatever this wooing scene was like in the lost, original text of *The Famous Victories of Henry V,* it has been made in Shakespeare's play to serve the theme of the king's two bodies: the dilemma of the man placed at a disadvantage in the sphere of personal relations by the fact of a corporate self.

Henry V:
English, Rhetoric, Theater

James L. Calderwood

The most difficult roles in Shakespeare are assigned to Oberon and
Ariel, for the latter is ordered by Prospero to "be subject / To no
sight but thine and mine" and Oberon is obliged by Shakespeare to
turn to the audience and announce "I am invisible." *Henry V* has a
role of similar difficulty. Although God does not appear in the list of
characters He nevertheless appears in the play. Or does He? When
Agincourt is safely won, Harry says:

> O God, thy arm was here;
> And not to us, but to thy arm alone,
> Ascribe we all! When, without strategem
> But in plain shock and even play of battle,
> Was ever known so great and little loss
> On one part and on the other? Take it, God,
> For it is none but thine!
>
> (4.8.111–17)

Agincourt presents us with the "plain shock and even play of battle"—that is, it is a genuine contest—and yet "God, thy arm was
here"—that is, it is not a genuine contest, for if God's arm was here,
it was here in behalf of the English. Somehow God manages to enact
a paradox of partisan impartiality. Perhaps the most that can be said
is that God has been discreet. He has made Agincourt as genuine a
contest as possible, not by abdicating His judgmental throne, but by

From *Metadrama in Shakespeare's Henriad:* Richard II *to* Henry V. © 1979 by the
Regents of the University of California. University of California Press, 1979.

eschewing ostentatious involvement. He has supplied no omens of victory to Harry, no portents or signs, offered no ghostly comforts in response to Harry's prayers, brought no legions into the field. Like Harry doffing regal ceremony to go among his troops on the eve of Agincourt as a mere man, God gives over divine ceremony and appears at Agincourt, if not as a "mere" God, at least as an unobtrusive one. So far as the audience can see, at any rate, Harry and the English are on their own.

To be present and yet invisible may come easily to gods and fairy kings—not so for dramatists. However commendable it might be for the playwright to remain impartial and divinely aloof from the internal factionalism of his work—even "paring his fingernails," as Stephen Dedalus would have it—he cannot help being present, at Agincourt or London, in the Forest of Arden or on the plains of Philippi. Like God, however, his presence may be either blatant or subtle. He can impose his dramatic order as conspicuously as Shakespeare does in Canterbury's speeches, blazoning his Englishness in an English cause; or he can aspire to a more genuine contest by generating complications, doubts, thematic oppositions—authentic antitheses against which his thesis must make its way. Shakespeare, I have argued, does what he can in this regard. Having loaded the dice to begin with, he does his best to unload them later. By compelling Harry to do battle in mortal doubt of God's inclinations, by holding God's judgment in abeyance until the dust has settled and the blood congealed, Shakespeare strives to achieve the dramatic equivalent of an ordeal by combat refereed by a concerned but distant God. In consequence, the English victory is both a divine gift—"O God, thy arm was here"—and a human achievement—"in plain shock and even play of battle." But the achievement comes first. Thus as Harry moves toward an earned kingship, *Henry V* moves toward an earned unity, making good its right to be so totally English.

More than that, perhaps, for we might want to argue that the play earns the right not merely to be English but also to be *in* English. At the end of the play we have a grand spousal of persons and nations, the political version of an overarching divine order, but of course behind the rituals of international harmony is poised the mailed fist of English nationalism. (Katherine, for instance, is not won over by the blandishments of a courtly lover—"I cannot so conjure up the spirit of love in her that he will appear in his true likeness," Harry tells Burgundy [5.2.315ff.]—but rather conquered by the siege of a soldier-king: "She is our capital demand, comprised / Within the fore-rank of our articles" [5.2.96–97]. The French are obliged to remember that Harry is titled not merely *Roi d'Angleterre* but also *Heritier de France*. Thus, when Burgundy, acting as though the forthcoming marriage were a private affair unrelated to national treaties and the past military engagements, conventionally remarks that love is blind, Harry sets the issue in its proper perspective: "It is so. And you may, some of you, thank love for my blindness, who cannot see many a fair French city for one fair French maid that stands in my way" [5.2.343–46].) By the same token, the linguistic version of divine order would be a marrying language that brings French and English under the same verbal roof, a unifying Esperanto presided over by God, best maker of all marriages. But there is no such language at the end of *Henry V,* and in its absence the King's English will serve. Indeed, it has served all along. Up until Katherine's English lesson in act 3, the French have all spoken English, as of course they must in an English play. Yet precisely because they must, the fact that they do passes largely unnoticed. In act 3, scene 2, where Jamy, Fluellen, and Macmorris convene to quarrel, Shakespeare asks us to observe that the dialects of Scotland, Wales, and Ireland may rasp and clash against each other but still address themselves to the English cause in harmony. However, while we watch the play advance toward a great military engagement between England and France, a test of dominance, we are not likely to realize that from the moment they have begun to speak the French have already suffered total defeat from Shakespeare's all-conquering English language. The first words spoken by the French king are "Thus comes the English will full power upon us" (2.4.1). He might with equal truth have said "Thus comes *English* with full power upon us," since by the all-compelling grace of an English playwright King Charles is unwittingly gifted with his enemies' speech. At Shakespeare's Agincourt there can be little hope for success for the French when even their battle cries must be issued in English.

I may seem to be making too much of what is simply an unavoidable necessity of English drama, a theatrical convention without which the play could not play. After all, the French in *Henry IV*—not to mention Greeks, Romans, Danes, Bohemians, Italians, in other plays—also speak English without being pursued by a cry of critics. Why seems it so particular with *Henry V?*

Henry V raises this linguistic issue primarily by means of

Katherine's language lesson in act 3, which is related to the general problem of partisan impartiality discussed earlier. Here again the dramatist plays the partisan, forcing the King's English upon both his play and the French, just as he Englishes divine order and makes straw men of his French characters. This Englishing of things, which happens whenever an author marshals his literary forces toward a predetermined victory, appears from one standpoint to be a dishonest stacking of the dramatic deck, but from another to be the indispensable price of artistic order, form, and unity. Parts, if they are to be parts, must be subdued if the whole is to be whole. And what could better illustrate the necessity of wholeness than the language in which a work is to be presented? If English speech did not unify *Henry V,* Bacon's "second curse" of man, Babel, would descend on the theater, rendering the play unintelligible through a clash of competing vernaculars.

So we concede, a bit unhappily, that the playwright must stack his linguistic deck no less than his thematic one and thereby incur the charge of dishonesty. Yet perhaps he need not be totally dishonest. At the very least he can avoid being an out-and-out knave by practicing his low dramatic shifts with a certain openness. He can confess to his audience that beguilement and dissembling are his stock in trade. Dramatic conflicts, he will remind us, are by nature recalcitrant; they will not resolve themselves of their own accord. If the playwright merely sets down on the fields of Agincourt a band of ragged and starving English, the French will swallow them whole. Christian history needs God's aid, English drama needs the English playwright's.

I argued earlier that Shakespeare raises this issue when he figures the withdrawal and return of the partisan playwright in the withdrawal and return of a partisan God. A truly high-minded, impartial God should not aid the English, but somehow does. An English playwright should not, in all honesty, aid the English, but, in all practicality, he is obliged to. Now, with respect to language, Shakespeare makes a similar point, announcing what he is artistically doing, what he cannot help doing. He introduces, *before* Agincourt, a scene in which the French princess takes a lesson in English speech— as though it were foreordained that Katherine's French must in the future give place to Harry's English.

Of course it *is* foreordained: history will not have it otherwise. In dramatizing this fact by means of the language lesson, even before the battle whose outcome will produce Katherine's marriage to Harry, Shakespeare underscores a larger fact: that he has compelled the French to speak Harry's English throughout the play. Through Katherine's English lesson Shakespeare addresses his audience somewhat as follows: "Let us be open with one another. The judicious among you will observe that Katherine will need no English if the French win at Agincourt. *If* the French win at Agincourt, then my play will contain, in this scene of the language lesson, a conspicuous irrelevance, an un-Aristotelean superfluity, as Ben Jonson will be quick to inform me. But of course I will not let the French win at Agincourt, because they *did* not win at Agincourt. And I will not let them speak French in my play, regardless of what they spoke in history, because the backward among you—glovers' sons from Stratford and the like—cannot understand French, let alone write it. So if I have not been quite fair to the French, at least I am being fair to you by exposing my dishonesty. However, let us not speak of dishonesty in this matter, but rather of how remarkably well I have instructed these haughty French, that they speak English, if not, my lords, as well as you, at least as well as I."

With something of this kind of openness Shakespeare becomes as honest as the theater will permit, and in this sense he earns the right to couch his play in English, especially during the final act. There we see Katherine's French yielding to Harry's English; for he, despite a few courteous assays at French, can find truth only in his native tongue: "Now, fie upon my false French! By mine honour, in true English, I love thee, Kate" (5.2.236–37). It is entirely fitting that a king who spent an unprincely youth learning all the dialects of England, who could "drink with any tinker in his own language" (*1 Henry IV,* 2.4.20), who studied "his companions / Like a strange tongue" (*2 Henry IV,* 4.4.68–69), and who learned his lessons so well that "when he speaks / The air, a chartered libertine, is still" (*Henry V,* 1.1.47–48)—that a king who has acquired such a command of English should subject all other accents and languages to its strict dominion. The round of oaths to be sworn at the end of the play (5.2.398–402) will be sworn, we can be sure, in English. The French will yield their words to the English conqueror even as they have yielded them to the English playwright from the beginning. What has been imposed from without, by Shakespeare, has been earned from within, by Harry.

Henry V ends with mention of this round of oaths whose purpose is to bind a man and a woman in marriage and two nations in peace. Shakespeare might have left it at this, ending on a note of triumph and reconciliation. Instead, however, he adds an epilogue in which he reminds us that Harry's triumph was short-lived. His successors not only broke the peace he so laboriously earned but also "lost France and made his England bleed" (l. 12). Given the stress in the final act upon the triumph of English as well as of *the* English, it is not merely the peace that is subverted by Shakespeare's epilogue but also the language in which that peace is framed—in which the entire play is framed. It is as though Shakespeare, not entirely satisfied with *Henry V,* advertises in his epilogue the impermanence of his achievement. The medium of dramatic expression has earned, it seems, only a short-term legitimacy. If these inferences are justified, we shall need to look more closely at the parallels between language and kingship.

Let me recapitulate. The breakdown of an ontological language in *Richard II* brings into divided focus both the lie and the metaphor as verbal symbionts. The *Henry IV* plays center in a fallen language whose once time-honored truths have been called in cynical doubt by a world governed at the top by the lying king at Westminster and at the bottom by the lying knight at Eastcheap. The young Prince Hal seems to accept the lie—not his father's kind, claiming to be more than he is, but his own kind, claiming to be less than he is—until he can wring from it a royal truth. More accurately, he begins with the appearance of a lie. What he has actually embraced is the doubleness of metaphor rather than the duplicity of the lie. If metaphor earns its truth by disguising itself as a lie, by claiming the name of another concept which it is not, then Hal makes his way to kingship metaphorically, by claiming the title of wastrel prince. This strategy, his descent into the clouds of Eastcheap in *Henry IV,* must pay off royally in *Henry V*—and of course does. Truancy miraculously issues in sense of duty, apparent self-indulgence as pious self-sacrifice. Once again, however, Harry finds himself confronted by metaphorical doubleness. He is not the perfect fusion of person and office, thing and name; he is not Richard II, the sacrosanct king of God's choice, but a mere man. On the other hand, he is not an outright lie, an illegitimate usurper of kingship; he is not Henry IV, but a king by direct lineal descent. Lacking credentials from God, he who once played the wastrel prince must now play the regal monarch. So young Harry plays King Henry V, not without a certain histrionic self-consciousness, until he can be assured of his title at Agincourt.

To play the king is to play the actor, for the king must have many roles in his repertoire. He must be able to play Henry VI, listening to the Archbishop and remaining oblivious to what the Church stands to gain from war with France. He must be able to play Richard III, affable and guileless as he springs his trap on the traitors. And Tamburlaine, crying down atrocities on the citizens of Harfleur. And Hotspur, covetous of honor at Agincourt and blunt-spoken soldier wooing Katherine. And as the learned Fluellen reminds us, he must play Alexander, killing his friend Cleitus at least figuratively, "for there is figures in all things." In these roles Harry acts marvelously well, and the militant English road company for which he stars prospers apace.

Now to militant kingship the parallel in language is militant speech—that is to say, rhetoric, the dominant verbal style in *Henry V*. Rhetoric in Harry's employ has not yet become, as it did in the sixteenth century, the language of ostentation, all gawds and tassels, but remains primarily functional and combative. Even when defined as the art of persuasion, rhetoric is a martial employment of words, its object being to conquer its verbal enemies through argument. And since conquest, as we have seen throughout *Henry V,* demands the ruthless subordination of individuals to the general cause, it follows that in the language of conquest words will be valued not in themselves but as instruments of political policy. "Turn him to any cause of policy," Canterbury says of the reformed Harry, and

> The Gordian knot of it he will unloose,
> Familiar as his garter; that when he speaks
> The air, a chartered libertine, is still,
> And the mute wonder lurketh in men's ears
> To steal his sweet and honeyed sentences;
> So that the art and practic part of life
> Must be the mistress of this theoric.
>
> (1.1.45–52)

The "sweet and honeyed" aspect of Harry's speech does not suggest rhetorical floweriness so much as the beehive theme of political order in which all parts serve the whole—as the royal honey of the king's language feeds men's ears, or as the "art and practic part of life" serves the "theoric" of policy. And to be sure, words in rhetorical service have something of the worker bee about them. Their job is not to glitter but to get things done. Thus, Harry's rhetoric is servanted to action. In its most strident employment, in his prebattle speeches, we have the Word as adrenalin. "Stiffen the sinews, summon up the blood," he cries before Harfleur (3.1.7); and after delivering his St. Crispian speech at Agincourt he concludes, "All things are ready, if our minds be so" (4.3.71). Rhetoric readies the mind, the mind readies the body, and a few unpromising English bodies, desperate with patriotism, go among the French like reapers.

However artificial, as in the considered hysteria of his exhortations before Harfleur, or bumbling, as in the near antispeech of his wooing of Katherine, Harry's speech accomplishes its rhetorical aims: it works. His stumbling French in the wooing scene reminds us that if he is not well-schooled in Katherine's language he most certainly is in his own. His studies of English in all its varieties and in all its classrooms, from Falstaff's taverns and highways to Hotspur's battlefields and Henry IV's court, have of course been also a studying of England herself. Through this self-imposed education Harry has made the King's English a composite of the speech of all England. As a result, the easy synecdoche by which the English king becomes "England"—as when King Charles commands his nobles to "Bar Harry England, that sweeps through our land" (3.5.48)—has in this king's case a more than usual claim to truth. Although Harry is careful to distinguish his ordinary self from his extraordinary office, as in the speech on ceremony, the high office nevertheless confers its magnitude upon him. The play's almost obsessive concentration on the rhetorical figure of the king—on Harry's voice addressing his courtiers, his soldiers, the French, Katherine—presents us not with the self-singing Richard II, nor with the multilingual nametrumpetings of Falstaff, but with the self-transcending language of corporate majesty. With all ideolects gathered in this King's English, Harry has become a linguistic version of H. C. Earwicker in his role of "Here Comes Everybody"—the personification of a manifold but unified Respublica.

Yet despite this air of success in Harry, there is that note of transitoriness in the epilogue, an implication that Harry's and Shakespeare's achievements are fleeting. Why Shakespeare chose to end on that note becomes clearer if we return to the Chorus and consider, as a parallel to the rhetorical issue, Shakespeare's preoccupation with the theatrical means at his disposal.

Henry V is surely the most self-conscious, even the most apol-

ogetic, of Shakespeare's plays. In the person of the Chorus the dramatist explores, exploits, but most of all laments the drawbacks of
theatrical presentation. How can this "cockpit hold / The vasty fields
of France," convey armies back and forth across the Channel, or
telescope the historical accomplishments of decades into "an hour-
glass"? These, one notes, are visual rather than verbal problems.
They would not arise if Shakespeare were writing an epic poem, as
many have wished, instead of an epic drama. They do not arise, for
instance, in such word-dominated histories as the *Henry VI* trilogy
or even *Richard II*. In those plays he is concerned less with the nature
of the stage than with that of speech. But now, with the Word fallen
into disrepute, he addresses himself to the nonverbal dimensions of
his art. If truth no longer resides in language, to be borne on speech
to the expectant ears of his audience, then it must be conveyed to
their eyes—though, alas, by the implausible makeshifts of theater:
"Yet sit and see, / Minding true things by what their mockeries be"
(prologue, act 4). Imparted by such scapegrace means, truth becomes
something of an embarrassment. When Agincourt is sadly abridged
to "four or five most vile and ragged foils / Right ill-disposed in
brawl ridiculous" (prologue, act 4), Shakespeare is not apt to speak
about drama holding the mirror of truth up to nature. What he does
speak of again and again, however, and always disparagingly, is the
purely functional nature of theater. Visual enactment is not a mimetic illusion of historical realities but an expedient, a device devoid
of truth in itself, rather shabby beside the glories it depicts, indeed a
mockery.

Yet the theater is not wholly without value and truth. The theatrical mockeries Shakespeare laments are analogous to the trappings
of kingship that the troubled King Harry debunks on St. Crispian's
Eve. Under the head of ceremony, the royal stage properties—

> the balm, the sceptre, and the ball,
> The sword, the mace, the crown imperial,
> The intertissued robe of gold and pearl,
> The farced title running 'fore the King,
> The throne he sits on, [and] the tide of pomp
> That beats upon the high shore of this world
> (4.1.277–82)

—may be "thrice-gorgeous," but at bottom they exist merely to
aggrandize the king and to create "awe and fear in other men." That

the ceremonies of kingship have no inherent truth is an admission Harry makes, to be sure, only in private soliloquy. However, his conduct at Agincourt, where he makes his "farced title" an authentic title, is consistent with his soliloquy. On the field he earns his kingship, not by robing himself in ceremony and thus distancing himself from his awed followers, but by putting off ceremony and addressing his soldiers as coequals in the martial enterprise: "For he that sheds his blood with me / Shall be my brother" (4.3.61–62). Only by donning the leather and mail of an English soldier does he earn the "intertissued robe of gold and pearl" of a true English king. Thus, it is not the charismatic Harry who triumphs at Agincourt but "We few, we happy few, we band of brothers" (4.3.60).

Like King Harry, Shakespeare recognizes the frailties of his own dramatic office, and if there is a Falstaffian ring to Harry's debunking of ceremony, so is there in Shakespeare's choral apologies for the debasements of theater. [Elsewhere] we saw Falstaff rising from apparent death and threatening to secede from *Henry IV* insofar as the play purports to be a realistic illusion of historical life. This internal uprising, which momentarily splits the play into a mimetic dimension occupied most prominently by the "dead" Hotspur and an artistic-theatrical dimension occupied most fully by the live Falstaff, was put down by Prince Hal, who alone inhabited both dimensions. Now, in the choral prologues of *Henry V*, Shakespeare has elevated Falstaff's revolt against the play into an official principle of the play. Over and again the Chorus makes Falstaff's divisive point about the purely theatrical and inadequate nature of what sets itself up as true history. Falstaff, nervously debating how dead Percy really was and how genuine his own pretence to death, said in effect to the audience, "I am the only true man here, since I confess that the play is a sham. The others, who pretend to be real, are counterfeiters and liars." Now it is Shakespeare who takes this line. The theater, he admits, has its limitations. One begins with that. Ben Jonson keeps insisting that we cannot shift scenes from England to France, squeeze Agincourt into a narrow theatrical O, or roll out the whole story of Harry's reign in a scant three hours. Not, at any rate, if we want to keep mimetic faith with reality. And Ben is absolute for mimesis. If he could, he would resurrect Harry and his fellows so that, playing themselves, they could reenact history before our eyes. Well, to be sure, that has its attractions:

O for a Muse of fire, that would ascend
The brightest heaven of invention,
A kingdom for a stage, princes to act,
And monarchs to behold the swelling scene!
Then should warlike Harry, like himself,
Assume the port of Mars; and at his heels,
Leashed in like hounds, should famine, sword, and fire
Crouch for employment. But.

(prologue, act 1)

It is, as Fluellen might say, an honest "but." Instead of attempting to foist theatrical illusions upon his audience in a sixteenth-century forerunner of epic cinema—"on-site filming with a cast of thousands!"—Shakespeare plainly acknowledges the limits of theater. Calling up the past to enact itself again is past the size of dreaming. For that original production God was the dramatist, but now we must make do with substitute playwrights sharked up from Stratford, partisan men given to the native tongue. God, best maker of marriages, is also best maker of reality; it is no part of dramatic wisdom to enter the lists with Him. How He manages His mortal and unruly materials toward providential ends defies understanding; how He frames His historical plot and yet leaves His actors freedom of will is sheer bafflement. *This* playwright, the Chorus keeps reminding us, operates otherwise. He deals of necessity in visual shifts and verbal craft, in disguises, techniques, beguilements. Whatever the credulous may think, to the discerning, this playwright's hand, unlike God's, is everywhere apparent; his wonders are performed not mysteriously but brazenly.

In short, this playwright works less like God shaping existential dramas than like a king fashioning plays of state—like King Harry, for instance, who has his repertory of political illusions to call on, who relies on ceremony to move the minds of his national audience, and who is conscious of the lack of inherent legitimacy in his methods and status. And therefore, as King Harry calls upon his followers to aid him as coequals at Agincourt, so the playwright Shakespeare calls upon his theatrical followers to aid him in recreating Agincourt. Indeed, in asking his audience to "eke out our performance with your mind" (prologue, act 3), he invites them to join with him as coauthors of the play. The theatrical victory that follows is, like Agincourt, the product of a collaborative enterprise. The unity of

English spirit on the battlefield is mirrored by the unity of English minds in the theater.

This victory—so truly theatrical in being achieved by the collective imagination of playwright, actors, and audience—marks the distance Shakespeare has come from the self-containment, the purely individual sovereignty of the lyric-narrative poet. It is his plainest admission of a truth he has grown to recognize more clearly from play to play—that the passage from poetry to drama involves a loss of creative independence, a sacrifice of self to the dramatic office that is analogous to the sacrifice of self to the political office made by King Henry.

One would like to stop on that note of dramatic triumph—but must, like Shakespeare, add an epilogue. With the fall of a language instinct with truth and value, a language envisaged in *Richard II,* Shakespeare has passed in the *Henry IV* plays through a period in which language seems entirely corrupt, a multitudinous lie, and on in *Henry V* to rhetorical speech, in which words acquire pragmatic value as instruments of action. Rhetoric as a response to the fall of language parallels Harry's reign as a response to the fall of kingship. That is, just as Harry, lacking divine-right sovereignty, earns his title to kingship through an ordeal by combat at Agincourt, so rhetoric, lacking the automatic sovereignty of poetry, earns its keep in action, substituting for inherent validity an achieved validity. Moreover, this conception of rhetoric as a pragmatic use of words has its analogue in Shakespeare's stress upon the theater as self-erasing technique—the purely instrumental makeshift by which the truths of English history are so imperfectly approached. Truth and value do not reside in theatrical presentation, any more than perfect circularity resides in a particular representation of a circle. *Henry V* acts upon the imagination of its audiences in such a way as to reach toward historical truths which it is, in itself, incapable of compassing.

As usual, Shakespeare is ahead of us. Thus, he reminds us in his epilogue that what King Harry achieved was soon lost, which suggests—if the kinship between king and dramatist holds true—that Shakespeare's own dramatic achievements are fugitive, that in deploying his artistic means toward shaping this nationalistic play he has found only a stop-gap solution to theatrical enigmas of enduring complexity. But that, after all, is the fate of means. Having no intrinsic value, they serve the needs of the occasion and then, as occasions change, fall from fashion. Rhetoric is cursed with built-in obsolescence; it inspires and, having attained its end, dissolves with all the finality of a Shakespearean performance. It may be revived, like *Henry V* itself, whenever war is again in favor and the hackles of the populace need raising. Another Harry, in the person of a Maurice Evans, for instance, may tour the battlefields of another war, crying "Once more unto the breach, dear friends, once more!" For the moment, in *Henry V,* Shakespeare may settle uneasily for that kind of verbal efficacy. But finding truth and meaning through one's art is a far cry from finding them *in* one's art. So the word serves its turn as rhetoric in *Henry V,* and epic drama serves its turn as stimulus of the patriotic imagination, and for a time the English, both in Harry's kingdom and in Shakespeare's theater, are bound in brotherhood. "Small time," the chorus says, "but in that small most greatly lived / This star of England" (epilogue). The small time of history has become even smaller on Shakespeare's stage. History is linear and unrepeatable, except in drama, and now that Shakespeare has freed his own drama from the eddying of *2 Henry IV,* it too has become linear and unrepeatable. The dramatic succession moves on, and we have not long to wait before *Hamlet* addresses itself by indirections to those familiar unresolved issues of theatrical illusion and poisoned speech.

Either/Or:
Responding to *Henry V*

Norman Rabkin

Henry V . . . has repeatedly elicited simple and wholehearted responses from its critics, interpretations that seem solidly based on total readings of a consistent whole. In this instance, however, sophisticated critics have not approached a single consensus; rather, they have gathered into rival camps which could hardly disagree more radically, and one finds two consensus views rather than one. For some critics, a recent writer [Karl P. Wentersdorf] remarks, "the play presents the story of an ideal monarch and glorifies his achievements; for them the tone approaches that of an epic lauding the military virtues. For others, the protagonist is a Machiavellian militarist who professes Christianity but whose deeds reveal both hypocrisy and ruthlessness; for them, the tone is predominantly one of mordant satire."

One way to deal with a play that provokes such conflicting responses is to try to find the truth somewhere between them. Another is to suggest that the dramatist couldn't make up his mind which side he wanted to come down on and left us a mess. A third is to interpret all the signals indicating one polar reading as intentional, and to interpret all the other signals as irrepressible evidence that Shakespeare didn't believe what he was trying to say. All of these strategies have been mounted against *Henry V*. All of them are wrong.

I am going to argue that in *Henry V* Shakespeare created a work

From *Shakespeare and the Problem of Meaning*. © 1981 by the University of Chicago. University of Chicago Press, 1981.

whose ultimate power is precisely the fact that it points in two opposite directions, virtually daring us to choose one of the two opposed interpretations it requires of us. In this deceptively simple play
Shakespeare experimented, more shockingly than elsewhere, with a
structure like the gestaltist's familiar drawing of a rare beast. [E. H.]
Gombrich describes the experience of that creature in memorable
terms:

> We can see the picture as either a rabbit or a duck. It is easy
> to discover both readings. It is less easy to describe what
> happens when we switch from one interpretation to the
> other. Clearly we do not have the illusion that we are
> confronted with a "real" duck or rabbit. The shape on the
> paper resembles neither animal very closely. And yet there
> is no doubt that the shape transforms itself in some subtle
> way when the duck's beak becomes the rabbit's ears and
> brings an otherwise neglected spot into prominence. I say
> "neglected," but does it enter our experience at all when
> we switch back to reading "duck"? To answer this ques-
> tion, we are compelled to look for what is "really there,"
> to see the shape apart from its interpretation, and this, we
> soon discover, is not really possible. True, we can switch
> from one reading to another with increasing rapidity; we
> will also "remember" the rabbit while we see the duck,
> but the more closely we watch ourselves, the more cer-
> tainly we will discover that we cannot experience alterna-
> tive readings at the same time. Illusion, we will find, is
> hard to describe or analyze, for though we may be intel-
> lectually aware of the fact that any given experience *must*
> be an illusion, we cannot, strictly speaking, watch our-
> selves having an illusion.
>
> (*Art and Illusion: A Study of the Psychology of Pictorial
> Representation*)

I

If one considers the context of *Henry V,* one realizes that the
play could scarcely have been anything but a rabbit-duck.

Henry V is, of course, not only a freestanding play but also the
last part of a tetralogy. Some years earlier, when his talent was up to
Titus Andronicus rather than to *Hamlet,* Shakespeare had had the nerve,

at the very beginning of his career, to shape the hopelessly episodic and unstructured materials of his chronicle sources not into the licensed formlessness of the history play his audience was used to— one recalls shapeless domestic chronicles like *Edward I* and *The Famous Victories of King Henry the Fifth* and foreign histories like *Tamburlaine* and *The Battle of Alcazar*—but rather into an integrated series of plays each satsifying as a separate unit but all deriving a degree of added power and meaning from being parts of a unified whole. It is scarcely credible that, with this tetralogy behind him, Shakespeare should have approached the matter of Lancaster without thinking of the possibility of a second unified series of plays. I can think of no other explanation for the fact that already in *Richard II* Hotspur—a character completely unnecessary to that play—has been made practically a generation younger than his model. The implication of the change is that in 1595 Shakespeare already intended a play about Prince Hal. And as one notices the innumerable cross-references and links and parallels among the plays of the second tetralogy, one feels more confidently than in the first cycle that such connections are not afterthoughts, backward indices in one play to what already existed in earlier plays, but evidence of conscious through-composition.

In any event, whether or not, as I think, Shakespeare knew four or five years beforehand that he would write *Henry V*, he certainly did know in 1599 that this drama would be the capstone to an edifice of plays tightly mortared to one another. And as with each part of *Henry IV*, he must have derived enormous power from the expectations his audience brought from the preceding plays. In two of the first three plays the audience had been confronted at the beginning with a set of problems that seemed solved by the end of the preceding play but had erupted in different forms as soon as the new play began. Thus the meaning of each of the plays subsequent to *Richard II* had been enriched by the audience's recognition of the emergence of old problems in a new guise. By the time the cycle reached *Henry V*, the recurrent and interlocking set of problems had become so complex that a reflective audience must have found it impossible to predict how the last play could possibly resolve them.

The unresolved thematic issue at the end of *Richard II* is the conflict of values embodied in the two kings who are its protagonists: Bolingbroke's talent as opposed to Richard's legitimacy; Bolingbroke's extraverted energy and calculating pursuit of power as opposed to Richard's imagination, inwardness, and sense of mortality. Richard's qualities make possible in him a spiritual life that reveals him as closer—even in his inadequacy—to the ideal figures of the comedies than is his successor, who nonetheless has the sheer force to survive and to rule to his country's advantage. If the play is structured to force one by the end to choose Bolingbroke as the better king—one need only contrast his disposition of Exton at the close with Richard's of Mowbray at the opening—one nevertheless finds one's emotions rather surprisingly committed to the failed Richard. *Richard II* thus poses a question that arches over the entire tetralogy: can the manipulative qualities that guarantee political success be combined in one man with the spiritual qualities that make one fully open and responsive to life and therefore fully human? Or, to put it more accurately, can political resourcefulness be combined with qualities more like those of an audience as it sees itself?

1 Henry IV moves the question to a new generation, asking in effect whether the qualities split between Richard and Bolingbroke can be united in Hal. And in the manner of a comedy, it suggests optimistically that indeed they can. Thus Hal's famous schematic stance between the appropriately dead Hotspur and a Falstaff equally appropriately feigning death indicates not so much a compromise between their incompatible values as the difference between Hal's ability to thrive in a world of process by employing time as an instrument and the oddly similar unwillingness of both Hotspur and Falstaff to do so.

For Hotspur, there is only the present moment. Even an hour is too long for life if honor is not its definition, and a self-destructive recklessness leads Hotspur to fight his battle at the wrong time, hoping naively to gain more glory. For Falstaff, time is equally irrelevant. Like the forest of Arden he needs no clock, since he has nowhere to go. He lives cyclically, recurring always to the same satisfactions of the same appetites, playing holiday every day, denying the scars of age and the imminence of death. Both of Hal's alter egos preposterously deny time, Hotspur to meet his death characteristically in midphrase—a phrase that Falstaff has already completed as "Food for powder"—and Falstaff to rise emblematically from his own death and shamelessly assert once again his will to live.

But Hal's affection for both men, so symmetrically expressed, suggests that he is in tune with something in each of them. Unlike his irascible father, but like both Hotspur and Falstaff, he is witty, ebulliently verbal, social, warmly responsive to others. For one illusory moment Shakespeare suggests the possibility of a public man who is privately whole. If the Prince's soliloquy has vowed an amputation he sees from the beginning as necessary, if the play extempore has ended in a suddenly heartbreaking promise to banish plump Jack and banish all the world, followed by the knock of the real world on the door, *1 Henry IV* nevertheless puts us in a comic universe in which Hal need never reject Falstaff in order to reach his father's side in the nick of time; it entices us with the hope of a political world transformed by the life of comedy.

But the end of *Henry IV, Part 1* marks only the halfway point, both in this massive tetralogy and in the study of Prince Hal, and *Part 2* brutally denies the comic optimism we might have expected to encounter once again. With the exception of Hotspur, all the ingredients of *Part 1* seem to be present again, and in some respects they seem stronger than ever. Falstaff is given a scene (2.4) perhaps even more endearing than Gadshill and its aftermath; he captivates Doll Tearsheet and, against her better knowledge, the Hostess. Ancient Pistol, who adds fresh attraction to the tavern world, performs one of the functions of the missing Hotspur by giving us a mocking perspective on the rhetoric and pretensions of the warrior.

And yet, despite all this and more, the effect of *Henry IV, Part 2* is to narrow possibilities. The rejection of Falstaff at its end seems to be both inevitable and right yet simultaneously seems to darken the world for which the paradise of the Boar's Head must be lost. Hotspur's absence, emphasized by the dramatic device of the series of rumors from which his father must pick it out at the beginning, roots out of the political world the atmosphere of youth, vigor, charm, and idealistic commitment that Hotspur almost alone had lent it before. And Hotspur's widow's just reproaches of her father-in-law stress the old man's ugly opportunism. Northumberland's nihilistic curse—

> Let heaven kiss earth! now let not Nature's hand
> Keep the wild flood confin'd! let order die!
> And let this world no longer be a stage
> To feed contention in a ling'ring act;
> But let one spirit of the first-born Cain
> Reign in all bosoms, that each heart being set

On bloody courses, the rude scene may end,
And darkness be the burier of the dead!
(1.1.153–60)

—makes clear the destructiveness of his rebellion, a thing far different from his late son's chivalric quest, and it creates an unequivocal sense that Hal has no choice but to oppose it as effectively as he can. No longer can we assent to Falstaff's observation, plausible in *Part 1,* that the rebels "offend none but the virtuous" (3.3.191), so that opposing them is almost a game. The harshness of the rebels' cause and company in *Part 2* demands of the audience a Hotspurian recognition that this is no world to play with mammets and tilt with lips.

Yet the attractiveness of the king's cause is reduced too. If in some moments—as in his sensitive meditation on the crown and his emotional final reunion with Hal—Henry IV is more likable in *Part 2* than he was in *Part 1,* he is no longer an active character (he doesn't even appear until the third act). And his place is filled by Prince John, as chilling a character as Shakespeare would ever create. Many a villain has more superficial charm than Hal's upright brother, and the priggish treachery by which Prince John overcomes the rebels arouses in us a distaste for political action, even when it is necessary, such as no previous moment in the plays has occasioned. If Shrewsbury implied that a mature politics was compatible with the joy of life lived fully and spontaneously, Gaultree now shows political responsibility as masked and sinister, an ally of death.

Given this characterization of the political world as joyless and cruel, one might expect Falstaff to carry the day. But, in fact, Shakespeare reduces him as much as he reduces the workaday world. It was a delicate paradox in *Part 1* that allowed us to admire Falstaff for his ridiculous denial of mortality—"They hate us youth"; "young men must live." Falstaff might worry about how he was dwindling away, but we had no fear of losing so eternal a companion. Or, to put it more accurately, we loved him for allaying such fears; for all his grumbling at Gadshill, he could run when he had to. But in *Part 2,* Falstaff is mired in gross physicality and the ravages of age, obsessed with his diseases and bodily functions, commanding that the Jordan be emptied, confirming as Doll caresses him ("I am old, I am old") his stage audience's observation that desire has outlasted performance. He is the same Falstaff, but the balance is altered.

As if for the reenactment of his great catechism on honor in *Part*

1, Falstaff is given a similar aria in *Part 2.* But the praise of sherris sack, funny as it is, is no more than a witty paean to alcohol, and a description at that of the mechanical operation of the spirit, whereas the rejection of honor in *Part 1* was convincing enough almost to undo our respect for anyone who subordinates life to ideals. Or again, the charge of foot for whom Falstaff is responsible in *Part 1* never becomes palpable, except to elicit his sympathetic "Food for powder," which puts him essentially on their side. In *Part 2,* however, we are introduced to his men by name, we see him choosing them (for the most self-serving reasons), and we are aware of the lives and families that Falstaff is ruining. No longer can we see him as the spokesman of life for its own sake; his ego is opportunistic, as not before, at the expense of others.

If the tavern world is no longer alluring for us, it is even more unattractive for Hal. Physically separated from Falstaff in *Part 2* as not in *Part 1,* the Prince is ready at any moment to express his discomfort, his guilt, his eagerness to be away. The flyting he carries on with Poins is unpleasant: if Hal feels so out of place consorting with commoners, why doesn't he simply stop doing it? We are tempted to agree with Warwick, who tells the King that Hal's only reason for spending time with his companions is his opportunistic scheme to use them:

> The Prince but studies his companions
> Like a strange tongue, where, to gain the language,
> 'Tis needful that the immodest word
> Be look'd upon and learnt, which once attain'd,
> Your Highness knows, comes to no further use
> But to be known and hated.
>
> (4.4.68–73)

The diseases literally corrupting Falstaff's body are endemic in *2 Henry IV.* Sickness and death pervade every element of the plot, virtually every scene, and it is no accident that it is here, not in *Part 1,* that we meet Justice Shallow, in senile debility only a step beyond the aged helplessness of Northumberland and the King. If the medium of action in *Part 1* was time seen as a hidden road that leads providentially toward a fulfilling moment, the medium of *Part 2* is repetitious and meaningless process drawing relentlessly to universal annihilation. Could one "read the book of fate," the moribund King reflects, one would have to

> see the revolution of the times
> Make mountains level, and the continent,
> Weary of solid firmness, melt itself
> Into the sea, and other times to see
> The beachy girdle of the ocean
> Too wide for Neptune's hips.
>
> (3.1.45–51)

What we recognize here is the time of the sonnets, of Ecclesiastes; and Warwick can cheer the King only by reminding him that at least time is inevitable. The sickness that infects both Falstaff and the body politic is the sickness of life itself, joyless and rushing to the grave. In such a world Prince Hal cannot play. He must do what he can for his kingdom, and that means casting Falstaff aside.

About the necessity for the rejection we are not given the chance to have any doubts: Falstaff, after all, has just told his companions that the law is his now, and, as A. R. Humphreys notes [in the Arden edition of *2 Henry IV*], Richard II had assured his own fall by making precisely this Nixonian claim. Yet we are forced to feel, and painfully, what an impoverishment of Hal's life the rejection causes. And we recognize another aspect of that impoverishment in the drive that moves Hal to take the crown prematurely from his dying father: his commitment to political power has impelled him, as the King recognizes bitterly, to a symbolic gesture that reveals an unconscious readiness for parricide. At the end of *Henry IV, Part 1,* Hal seemed able to accommodate all of England into his family as he moved toward its symbolic fatherhood. By the end of *Part 2,* in order to become king of England he has reached out to murder both of his fathers.

II

If we fancy ourselves arriving, on an afternoon in 1599, for the first performance of *Henry V,* we must imagine ourselves quite unsure of what to expect. Some months earlier the epilogue to *2 Henry IV* had promised that "our humble author will continue the story, with Sir John in it, and make you merry with fair Katherine of France, where (for any thing I know) Falstaff shall die of a sweat, unless already 'a be kill'd with your hard opinions; for Oldcastle died[a] martyr, and this is not the man." This disingenuous come-on allows for both sympathetic and hostile readings of Falstaff, while disclaiming any knowledge of the author's intentions. But the plays that precede *Henry V* have aroused such ambivalent expectations that the question of the epilogue is trivial. If *Henry V* had followed directly on *1 Henry IV,* we might have expected to be made merry by the comedy such critics as Dover Wilson have taken that play to be, for we have seen a Hal potentially larger than his father, possessing the force that politics requires without the sacrifice of imagination and range that Bolingbroke has had to pay. But *Part 2* has told us that *Part 1* deceived us, for the day has had to come when Hal, no longer able to live in two worlds, would be required to make his choice, and the Prince has had to expel from his life the very qualities that made him better than his father. Have we not, after *Part 2,* good reason to expect in the play about Hal's kingship the study of an opportunist who has traded his humanity for his success, covering over the ruthlessness of the politician with the mere appearance of fellowship that his past has endowed him with? Surely this is what Goddard means when he calls Henry V "the golden casket of *The Merchant of Venice,* fairer to a superficial view than to a more searching perception."

As we watch the Chorus stride across the stage of the Curtain Theater, then, we are ready for one of two opposed presentations of the reign of the fifth Henry. Perhaps we hope that the play now beginning will resolve our doubts, set us right, give us a single gestalt to replace the antithetical images before our mind's eye. And that, as is demonstrated by the unequivocal interpretations good critics continue to make, is exactly the force of the play. We are made to see a rabbit or a duck. In fact, if we do not try obsessively to cling to memories of past encounters with the play, we may find that each time we read it it turns from one shape to the other, just as it so regularly does in production. I want to show that *Henry V* is brilliantly capable of being read, fully and subtly, as each of the plays the two parts of *Henry IV* had respectively anticipated. Leaving the theater at the end of the first performance, some members of the audience knew that they had seen a rabbit, others a duck. Still others, and I would suggest that they were Shakespeare's best audience, knew uneasily that they did not know what to think.

III

Think of *Henry V* as an extension of *1 Henry IV*. For the generation who came to know it under the spell of Olivier's great film, it is hard to imagine *Henry V* any other way, but Olivier's distortions, deletions, and embellishments only emphasized what is already in the play. The structure of the entire cycle has led from the beginning of conflict in a quarrel to its end in a wedding, from the disruption of royal power to its unchallenged reassertion. If *Richard II* at the beginning transformed the normally episodic chronicle form into tragedy, *Henry V* at the end turns it into comedy: the plot works through the troubles of a threatening world to end in marriage and the promise of a green world. Its protagonist, like Benedick returned to Messina, puts aside military exploits for romance, and charms even his enemies with his effervescent young manhood. Its prologue insists, as the comedies always do, on the importance of imagination, a faculty which Bolingbroke, wise to the needs of a tragic world, had rejected in *Richard II* as dangerous. And, as in all romantic comedy, providence guides the play's events to their desired conclusion.

To be sure, Olivier's camera and Walton's music prettied up the atmosphere, transporting their war-weary audience to the fairy-tale world of the Duc de Berry. But they found their cues in the play—in the Chorus's epic romanticizations of land and sea, his descriptions of festooned fleets and nocturnal campfires and eager warriors, and his repeated invitations to imagine even more and better. Nor did Olivier invent his film's awe at the spectacle of the past. In *Henry V*, as nowhere before in the tetralogy, Shakespeare excites us by making us conscious that we are privileged to be watching the very moments at which event transforms itself into history:

> MONTJOY: The day is yours.
> KING HENRY: Praised be God, and not our strength, for
> it!
> What is this castle call'd that stands hard by?
> MONTJOY: They call it Agincourt.
> KING HENRY: Then call we this the field of Agincourt,
> Fought on the day of Crispin Crispianus.
>
> (4.8.86–91)

Ultimately, it was not Olivier's pictures but the play's language that made his *Henry V* so overwhelming; the rhetoric of the play is extraordinary, unprecedented even in Shakespeare. Think, for example, of the King's oration to his troops on Saint Crispin's day (4.3.19–67). Thematically, of course, the speech is a tour de force, subjecting motifs from the tetralogy to Aeschylean transmutations. Like the dying John of Gaunt, Harry is inspired by a vision of England, but one characteristically his own, made as romantic by the fantasy of neighborhood legionnaires and domestic history lessons as by the magical names of England's leaders. Unlike Richard II, Harry disprizes trappings, "outward things." Like Hotspur, he cares only about honor and wants to fight with as few troops as possible in order to acquire more of it: "the fewer men, the greater share of honor." Like Falstaff, he is finicky about the kind of men he adventures with: "we would not die in that man's company / That fears his fellowship to die with us." Again like Falstaff, he thinks of the "flowing cups" to come when the day's work is done, and sees the day's events in festival terms. Gaily doing battle on the feast of Crispian, he is literally playing at war like Hotspur, paradoxically uniting the opposed principles of the two most enchanting characters of the cycle.

Such echoes and allusions give Henry's speech a satisfying finality, a sense of closure. He is the man we have been waiting for, the embodiment of all the virtues the cycle has made us prize, without the vices that had accompanied them before. "He is as full of valor as of kindness," we have heard just before the speech, "Princely in both," and the Crispin's day exhortation demonstrates precisely the combination of attributes that Sherman Hawkins has pointed out as belonging to the ideal monarch postulated by Elizabethan royalism. But even more powerful than its thematic content is the stunning rhetoric of the King's tirade: its movement from the King's honor to his people's; its crescendo variations on Saint Crispin's day, reaching their climax in the last line; its rhythmic patterns expanding repeatedly from broken lines to flowing periods in each section and concluding climactically in the coda that begins "We happy few"; its language constantly addressed to the pleasures, worries, and aspirations of an audience of citizens. As Michael Goldman perceptively argues, such a speech almost literally moves us. We recognize it as a performance; we share the strain of the king's greatness, the necessary effort of his image-projecting. "We are thrilled," Goldman says, "because he is brilliantly meeting a political challenge that has been spelled out for us. . . . It is a moment when he must respond to the unspoken needs of his men, and we respond to his success as we do when a political leader we admire makes a great campaign speech: we love him for his effectiveness."

The fourth act of *Henry V,* in the third scene of which this speech has its place, is a paradigm of the King's virtues. It begins with the Chorus's contrast between the "confident and over-lusty French" and the thoughtful and patient Englishmen at their watchful fires on the eve of Agincourt, visited by their generous, loving, brave, and concerned royal captain—"a little touch of Harry in the night." The act moves, first through contrasting scenes in the two camps, then through confrontations of various sorts between the opposing sides, to the victory at Agincourt and the King's call for the charitable treatment of the dead as he announces his return to England. In the course of the act we see Harry, constantly contrasted to the stupid and corrupt French, in a triumphant show of bravery and high spirits. But we see him also in a kind of inwardness we have seldom observed in his father, listening as neither Richard II or Henry IV could have done to the complaints and fears of a common soldier who knows what kings impose on their subjects that the kings themselves do not have to risk. His response is a soliloquy as powerful in its thematic and rhetorical complexity as the public address we have just considered (4.41.230–84).

In some respects this soliloquy, which precedes by only a few moments the Crispin's day speech, is the thematic climax of the entire tetralogy, showing us that at last we have a king free of the crippling disabilities of his predecessors and wise in what the plays have been teaching. Recognizing that all that separates a king from private men is ceremony, Harry has escaped Richard's tragic confusion of ceremony with reality: "Is not the King's name twenty thousand names?" Unwittingly reenacting his father's insomniac soliloquy in the third act of *2 Henry IV,* Harry too longs for the heart's ease of the commoner. But where the old King could conclude only, "Uneasy lies the head that wears a crown," recurring despairingly to his posture of perennial guiltiness and to his weary sense of mortality, his young son ends by remembering his responsibility, his life of service, and sees that—"what watch the King keeps to maintain the peace"—as the defining mark of the king. Moreover, in his catechistic questioning of ceremony Harry shows that he has incorporated Falstaff's clear-sightedness: like honor in Falstaff's catechism, ceremony consists only in what is conferred by others, bringing no tangible good to its bearer, unable to cure disease, no more than a proud dream. But the lesson is not only Falstaff's; for, at the opposite end of the tetralogy, before Hal ever entered the scene, a young Bolingbroke had anticipated his son's "Thinks thou the fiery fever will go out / With titles blown from adulation?" with a similar repudiation of comforting self-deception:

> O, who can hold a fire in his hand
> By thinking of the frosty Caucasus?
> Or cloy the hungry edge of appetite
> By bare imagination of a feast?
> (*Richard II*, 1.3.294–97)

These multiple allusions force us to see in Henry V the epitome of what the cycle has taught us to value as best in a monarch, indeed in a man; and the King's ability to listen to the soldier Williams and to hear him suggests, like his subsequent fooling with Fluellen in the same fourth act, a king who is fully a man. All that is needed to complete him is mature sexuality, scarcely hinted at in the earlier portraits of Hal, and the wooing of Princess Katherine in the fifth act brings finality to a lively portrayal of achieved manhood, a personality integrated in itself and ready to bring unity and joy to a realm that has suffered long from rule by men less at ease with themselves and less able to identify their own interests with those of their country. It was such a response to *Henry V* that led me years ago to write:

> In only one play in his entire career does Shakespeare seem bent on making us believe that what is valuable in politics and in life can successfully be combined in a ruler as in his state. . . . There can be no doubt that [the play] is infectiously patriotic, or that the ideal of the harmonious commonweal . . . reflects the highest point of Shakespeare's civic optimism. And Henry is clearly presented as the kind of exemplary monarch that neither Richard II nor Henry IV could be, combining the inwardness and the sense of occasion of the one and the strength of the other with a generous humanity available to neither. . . . In *Henry V* Shakespeare would have us believe what hitherto his work in its genre has denied, that in the real world of the chronicles a man may live who embodies the virtues and experiences the fortunes of the comic hero.

Reading the play thus optimistically, I had to note nevertheless how many readers respond otherwise to it, and I went on to observe that the play casts so many dark shadows—on England after Agincourt, for instance—that one can scarcely share its optimism, and that "in this respect *Henry V* is the most melancholy of the history plays." But I have now come to believe that my acknowledgment of that darker aspect of the play hardly suggested the terrible subversiveness with which Shakespeare undermines the entire structure.

IV

Taking the play, as we have just done, to be an extension of the first part of *Henry IV,* we are almost inevitably propelled to optimism. Taking it as the sequel of the second part of *Henry IV,* we are led to the opposite view held by critics as diverse as H. C. Goddard, Roy W. Battenhouse, Mark Van Doren, and H. M. Richmond. Think of those dark shadows that cloud the comedy. The point of the stock ending of romantic comedy is, of course, its guarantee of the future: marriage secures and reinvigorates society while promising an extension of its happiness into a generation to come. Like *A Midsummer Night's Dream, Henry V* ends in a marriage whose blessing will transform the world:

> KING HENRY: Now welcome, Kate; and bear me witness all,
>   That here I kiss her as my sovereign queen. *Flourish.*
> QUEEN ISABEL: God, the best maker of all marriages,
>   Combine your hearts in one, your realms in one!
>   As man and wife, being two, are one in love,
>   So be there 'twixt your kingdoms such a spousal,
>   That never may ill office, or fell jealousy,
>   Which troubles oft the bed of blessed marriage,
>   Thrust in between the [paction] of these kingdoms,
>   To make divorce of their incorporate league;
>   That English may as French, French Englishmen,
>   Receive each other. God speak this Amen!
> ALL: Amen!
> KING HENRY: Prepare we for our marriage; on which day,
>   My Lord of Burgundy, we'll take your oath,

And all the peers', for surety of our leagues.
Then shall I swear to Kate, and you to me,
And may our oaths well kept and prosp'rous be!
Sennet. Exeunt.

We don't really know very much about what was to happen in
Theseus's Athens. But we know a good deal about Plantagenet England; and in case any member of the audience has forgotten a history as familiar to Elizabethans as our Civil War is to us, the Chorus
appears immediately to remind them—both of what would soon
happen, and of the fact that they have already seen a cycle of
Shakespearean plays presenting that dismal story. The shock of the
suddenly depressing reversal of all the optimism suggested by the
first ending is all the more intense because the Chorus's speech
promises in its opening lines to continue in the celebratory vein of
the last scene, only to turn unexpectedly in its last four lines to harsh
negation:

Small time, but in that small most greatly lived
This star of England. Fortune made his sword;
By which the world's best garden he achieved,
And of it left his son imperial lord.
Henry the Sixt, in infant bands crown'd King
Of France and England, did this king succeed;
Whose state so many had the managing,
That they lost France, and made his England bleed;
Which oft our stage hath shown; and for their sake,
In your fair minds let this acceptance take.

"But if the cause be not good," Williams muses on the eve of
Agincourt (4.1.134–42), "the King himself hath a heavy reckoning
to make, when all those legs and arms, and heads, chopp'd off in a
battle, shall join together at the latter day and cry all, 'We died at
such a place'—some swearing, some crying for a surgeon, some
upon their wives left poor behind them, some upon the debts they
owe, some upon their children rawly left. I am afeard there are few
die well that die in a battle." Replying to Williams, the King insists
that the state of a man's soul at the moment of his death is his own
responsibility. Though to Samuel Johnson this appeared "a very just
distinction," the King's answer evades the issue: the suffering he is
capable of inflicting, the necessity of being sure that the burden is

imposed for a worthy cause. The end of the play bleakly implies that there is no such cause; all that Harry has won will be lost within a generation. The epilogue wrenches us out of the paradise of comedy into the purgatory of Shakespearean time, where we incessantly watch

> the hungry ocean gain
> Advantage on the kingdom of the shore,
> And the firm soil win of the wat'ry main,
> Increasing store with loss, and loss with store.

Contemplation of "such interchange of state, / Or state itself confounded to decay" (Sonnet 64) does not incline one toward attempting apocalyptic action. It is more likely to encourage reflections like those of Henry IV about the "revolution of the times," or of Falstaff in the very next scene of *2 Henry IV:* "let time shape, and there an end" (3.2.332).

But the implication that the cause is not good disturbs us well before the aftermath of Agincourt. The major justification for the war is the Archbishop of Canterbury's harangue on the Salic law governing hereditary succession, a law the French are said to have violated. The Archbishop's speech to the King follows immediately on his announcement to the Bishop of Ely that he plans to propose the war as a means of alleviating a financial crisis in the church. The speech itself is long, legalistic, peppered with exotic genealogies impossible to follow; its language is involuted and syntactically loose. The very qualities that makes its equivalent in Shakespeare's sources an unexceptionable instrument of statecraft make it sound on the stage like doubletalk, and Canterbury's conclusion that it is "as clear as is the summer's sun" that King Henry is legitimate king of France is a sardonic bit of comedy. Olivier, unwilling to let on that Shakespeare might want us to be less than convinced, turned the episode into farce at the expense of the Elizabethan actor playing the part of Canterbury. Denied the resources of a subsidized film industry, scholars who want to see the war justified must praise the speech on the basis of its content, ignoring its length and style. Thus in the words of one scholar, "the Archbishop discharges his duty faithfully, as it stands his reasoning is impeccable apart from any warrant given by the precedent of Edward III's claims. Henry is not initiating aggression" (J. H. Walter, Arden edition of *Henry V*). Bradley, whose argument the critic just cited was answering, is truer to the situation:

"Just as he went to war chiefly because, as his father told him, it was the way to keep factious nobles quiet and unite the nation, so when he adjures the Archbishop to satisfy him as to his right to the French throne, he knows very well that the Archbishop *wants* the war, because it will defer and perhaps prevent what he considers the spoliation of the Church" ("The Rejection of Falstaff," in *Oxford Lectures on Poetry,* 2d ed.).

J. H. Walter points out that Henry's reaction to the insulting gift of tennis balls from the Dauphin is strategically placed, as not in the play's sources, after the King has already decided to go to war, and he argues that Shakespeare thus "uses [the incident] to show Henry's christian self-control." This is an odd description of a speech which promises to avenge the gift with the griefs of "many a thousand widows" for their husbands, of mothers for their sons, and even of "some [who] are yet ungotten and unborn" (1.2.284–87). Since the tennis balls are a response to a challenge already issued (Henry's claim that France is his by rights) the King's rage seems just a little self-righteous. Henry's insistence throughout the scene that the Archbishop reassure him as to his right to make the claim insures our suspicion that the war is not quite the selfless enterprise other parts of the play tempt us to see.

Our suspicions are deepened by what happens later. H. C. Goddard has left us a devastating attack on Henry V as Shakespeare's model Machiavellian. Goddard's intemperate analysis, as right as it is one-sided, should be read by everyone interested in the play. I want to quote only one brief excerpt, his summary of the "five scenes devoted to" the battle of Agincourt; the account will be particularly useful to those who remember the battle scenes in Olivier's film.

1. Pistol captures a Frenchman.
2. The French lament their everlasting shame at being worsted by slaves.
3. Henry weeps at the deaths of York and Suffolk and orders every soldier to kill his prisoners.
4. Fluellen compares Henry with Alexander and his rejection of Falstaff to the murder of Cleitus. Henry, entering angry, swears that every French prisoner, present and future, shall have his throat cut. . . . The battle is over. The King prays God to keep him honest and breaks his word of honor to Williams.

5. Henry offers Williams money by way of satisfaction, which Williams rejects. Word is brought that 10,000 French are slain and 29 English. Henry gives the victory to God.

If Shakespeare had deliberately set out to deglorify the Battle of Agincourt in general and King Henry in particular it would seem as if he could hardly have done more.

Admittedly, Goddard's analysis is excessively partisan. He ignores the rhetoric we have admired, he sees only the King's hypocrisy on Agincourt eve, and he refuses the Chorus's repeated invitations to view the war as more glorious than what is shown. But the burden of Goddard's argument is difficult to set aside: the war scenes reinforce the unpleasant implications of the Salic law episode. Consider the moment, before the great battle, when the King bullies the citizens of Harfleur, whose surrender he demands, with a rapacious violence that even J. H. Walter does not cite as an instance of "Henry's christian self-control":

> If I begin the batt'ry once again,
> I will not leave the half-achieved Harflew
> Till in her ashes she lies buried.
> The gates of mercy shall be all shut up,
> And the flesh'd soldier, rough and hard of heart,
> In liberty of bloody hand, shall range
> With conscience wide as hell, mowing like grass
> Your fresh fair virgins and your flow'ring infants.
> What is it then to me, if impious War,
> Arrayed in flames like to the prince of fiends,
> Do with his smirch'd complexion all fell feats
> Enlink'd to waste and desolation?
> What is't to me, when you yourselves are cause,
> If your pure maidens fall into the hand
> Of hot and forcing violation?
> What reign can hold licentious wickedness
> When down the hill he holds his fierce career?
>
> (3.3.7–23)

In such language as Tamburlaine styled his "working words," the King, like the kind of aggressor we know all too well, blames the rapine he solicits on his victims. The alacrity of his attack makes one understand Yeats's description of Henry V as "a ripened Fortinbras";

its sexual morbidity casts a disquieting light on the muted but un-
mistakable aggressiveness of his sexual assault on Katherine in the
fifth act.

Henry's killing of the French prisoners inspires similar uneasiness. Olivier justified this violation of the putative ethics of war by
making it a response to the French killing of the English luggage
boys, and one of the most moving moments in his film was the
King's passionate response: "I was not angry since I came to
France / Until this instant." After such a moment one could hardly
fault Henry's

> Besides, we'll cut the throats of those we have,
> And not a man of them that we shall take
> Shall taste our mercy.
>
> (4.7.55–65)

In the same scene, indeed, Gower observes that it was in response to
the slaughter of the boys that "the King, most worthily, hath caus'd
every soldier to cut his prisoner's throat. O, 'tis a gallant king!" But
the timing is wrong: Gower's announcement came *before* the King's
touching speech. In fact, Shakespeare had presented the decision to
kill the prisoners as made at the end of the preceding scene, and while
in the source it has a strategic point, in the play it is simply a response
to the fair battlefield killing of some English nobles by the French.
Thus, the announcement comes twice, first as illegitimate, second as
if it were a spontaneous outburst of forgivable passion when it actually is not. In such moments as this we feel an eloquent discrepancy
between the glamor of the play's rhetoric and the reality of its action.

Henry IV, Part 1 is "about temperance and fortitude," *Part 2* is
"about wisdom and justice," and Shakespeare's "plan culminates in
Henry V." So argues Sherman Hawkins. "Henry's right to France—
and by implication England—," he claims, "is finally vindicated by
a higher power than the Archbishop of Canterbury." God's concern
that France be governed by so ideal a monarch culminates, of course,
in the ruins so movingly described in act 5 by the Duke of Burgundy, to whose plea the King responds like the leader of a nation of
shopkeepers with a demand that France "buy [the] peace" it wants
according to a contract Henry just happens to have had drawn up.
What follows is the King's coarse wooing of his captive princess,
with its sexual innuendo, its repeated gloating over Henry's possession of the realm for which he sues, and its arch insistence on his

sudden lack of adequate rhetoric. Johnson's judgment is hardly too severe: the King "has neither the vivacity of Hal nor the grandeur of Henry. . . . We have here but a mean dialogue for princes; the merriment is very gross, and the sentiments are very worthless."

Henry's treatment of France may suggest to the irreverent that one is better off when providence does not supply such a conqueror. And his impact on England is scarcely more salubrious. The episodes in which the King tricks Fluellen and terrifies Williams recall the misbehavior of the old Hal, but with none of the old charm and a lot more power to do hurt. In *2 Henry IV* it was the unspeakable Prince John who dealt self-righteously with traitors; in *Henry V* it is the King himself. In the earlier plays wars were begun by others; in *Henry V* it is the King himself, as he acknowledges in his soliloquy, having apparently decided not to go on pinning the blame on the Archbishop of Canterbury. And England must pay a high price for the privilege of the returning veterans to show their wounds every October 25.

We do not have to wait for the epilogue to get an idea of it. At the end of act 4, as we saw, the King calls for holy rites for the dead and orders a return to England. The Chorus to the ensuing act invites us to imagine the King's triumphant return, his modesty, and the outpouring of grateful citizens. But in the next scene we find ourselves still in France, where Fluellen gives Pistol, last of the company of the Boar's Head, the comeuppance he has long fended off with his shield of preposterous language. Forced to eat his leek, Pistol mutters one last imprecation ("all hell shall stir for this"), listens to Gower's final tongue-lashing, and, alone on the stage at last, speaks in soliloquy:

> Doth Fortune play the huswife with me now?
> News have I that my Doll is dead i' th' spittle
> Of a malady of France.
> And there my rendezvous is quite cut off.
> Old do I wax, and from my weary limbs
> Honor is cudgell'd. Well, bawd I'll turn,
> And something lean to cutpurse of quick hand.
> To England will I steal, and there I'll steal;
> And patches will I get unto these cudgell'd scars,
> And [swear] I got them in the Gallia wars.
> (5.1.80–89)

The pun on "steal" is the last faint echo of the great Falstaff scenes, but labored and lifeless now as Pistol's pathetic bravura. Pistol's exit occasioned Johnson's most affecting critical comment: "The comick scenes of the history of Henry the Fourth and Fifth are now at an end, and all the comick personages are now dismissed. Falstaff and Mrs. Quickly are dead; Nym and Bardolph are hanged; Gadshill was lost immediately after the robbery; Poins and Peto have vanished since, one knows not how; and Pistol is now beaten into obscurity. I believe every reader regrets their departure." But our regret is for more than the end of some high comedy: it is for the reality of the postwar world the play so powerfully conjures up—soldiers returned home to find their jobs gone, falling to a life of crime in a seamy and impoverished underworld that scarcely remembers the hopes that accompanied the beginnings of the adventure.

It is the "duty of the ruler," Hawkins says, "to make his subjects good." For the failure of his subjects, the play tells us, we must hold Henry V and his worthless war responsible. Unsatisfactory though he was, Henry IV was still the victim of the revolution of the times, and our ultimate attitude toward him, hastened to death as he was by the unconscious ambition of his own son, took a sympathetic turn like that with which we came at the end to regard the luckless Richard. But Henry V, master manipulator of time, has by the end of the cycle immersed himself in the destructive element. The blows he has rained on his country are much more his than those of any enemy of the people, and all he has to offer his bleeding subjects for the few years that remain is the ceremonial posture which he himself has earlier had the insight to contemn. Like the Edmund of *King Lear,* another lusty and manipulative warrior who wins, woos, and dies young, Henry might have subscribed himself "in the ranks of death."

V

This, then, is the problem of *Henry V*. Along the way I have cited some critics who see an exemplary Christian monarch, one who has attained, "in the language of Ephesians, both the 'age' and 'stature' of a perfect man (Hawkins)." And I have cited others who see "the perfect Machiavellian prince," a coarse and brutal highway robber (Goddard). Despite their obvious differences, these rival views are essentially similar, for each sees only a clear gestalt. I hope that simply by juxtaposing the two readings I have shown that each of them, persuasive as it may be, is reductive, requiring that we exclude too much to hold it.

Other positions, as I suggested at the outset, are possible. One of them began with Samuel Johnson, was developed by some of the best critics of a generation ago, among them Tillyard and Van Doren, and found its most humane expression in a fine essay in which Una Ellis-Fermor argued that by 1599 Shakespeare no longer believed what he found himself committed to create. Having achieved his portrait of the exemplary public man, she suggests, Shakespeare was already on the verge of a series of plays that would ever more vexingly question the virtue of such virtue. Never again would Shakespeare ask us to sympathize with a successful politician, instead relegating such men to the distasteful roles of Fortinbras, Octavius (in both *Julius Caesar* and *Antony and Cleopatra*), Alcibiades, and Aufidius. Malcolm is a terrible crux in *Macbeth*. Between quarto and folio texts of *Lear,* Shakespeare or his redactor is unable to devote enough attention to the surviving ruler of Britain for us to be able to identify him confidently. The governance of Cyprus and Venice is a slighter concern in *Othello* than the embroidery on the Moor's handkerchief. "Not even Shakespeare," Johnson said of what he considered the failure of the last act of *Henry V,* "can write well without a proper subject. It is a vain endeavor for the most skilful hand to cultivate barrenness, or to paint upon vacuity."

A. P. Rossiter's seminal essay, "Ambivalence—the Dialectic of the Histories," sensitively shows Shakespeare's double view of every important issue in the earlier history plays. But when he comes to *Henry V,* Rossiter abandons his schema and decides that Shakespeare momentarily lost his interest in a problematic view of reality and settled for shallow propaganda on behalf of a character whom already he knew well enough to loathe. But *Henry V* is too good a play for criticism to go on calling it a failure. It has been performed successfully with increasing frequency in recent years, and critics have been treating it with increasing respect.

A third response has been suggested by some writers of late: *Henry V* is a subtle and complex study of a king who curiously combines strengths and weaknesses, virtues and vices. One is attracted to the possibility of regarding the play unpolemically. Shakespeare is not often polemical, after all, and a balanced view allows for the inclusion of both positive and negative features in an analysis of the protagonist and the action. But sensitive as such analysis can be, it is oddly unconvincing, for two strong reasons. First, the cycle has led us to expect stark answers to simple and urgent questions. Is a particular king good or bad for England? Can one be a successful public man and retain a healthy inner life? Has Hal lost or gained in the transformation through which he changes name and character? Does political action confer any genuine benefit on the polity? What is honor worth, and who has it? The mixed view of Henry characteristically appears in critical essays that seem to fudge such questions, to see complication and subtlety where Shakespeare's art forces us to demand commitment, resolution, answers. Second, no real compromise is possible between the extreme readings I have claimed the play provokes. Our experience of the play resembles the experience Gombrich claims for viewers of the trick drawing: "We can switch from one reading to another with increasing rapidity; we will also 'remember' the rabbit while we see the duck, but the more closely we watch ourselves, the more certainly we will discover that we cannot experience alternative readings at the same time."

VI

What I have been describing in *Henry V* sounds very much like what Empson seems to announce in his seventh type of ambiguity, though as usual he is talking about words rather than about anything so grand as a whole play:

> An example of the seventh type of ambiguity . . . occurs when the two meanings of the word, the two values of the ambiguity, are the two opposite meanings defined by the context, so that the total effect is to show a fundamental division in the writer's mind.

If what happens in *Henry V* is a version of the fundamental ambiguity that many critics have found at the center of the Shakespeare vision, it is nevertheless significantly different here. Such ambiguity is not a theme or even the most important fact in many plays in which it figures. I have argued elsewhere that it is extraordinarily important in *Hamlet,* but to reduce *Hamlet* to a statement about "complementarity" is to remove its life. Though one perceives it informing plays as different from one another as *A Midsummer Night's Dream* and *King Lear,* one cannot say that it is what they are "about," and readings of Shakespearean plays as communicating only ambiguity are as arid as readings in which the plays are seen to be about appearance and reality; just so in Empson ambiguity often seems to be merely a trope, a stock tool in the poet's kit.

In *Henry V,* however, Shakespeare's habitual recognition of the irreducible complexity of things has led him, as it should lead his audience, to a point of crisis. Since by now virtually every other play in the canon has been called a problem play, let me add *Henry V* to the number. Suggesting the necessity of radically opposed responses to a historical figure about whom there would seem to have been little reason for anything but the simplest of views, Shakespeare leaves us at a loss. Is it any wonder that *Julius Caesar* would follow in a few months, where Shakespeare would present one of the defining moments in world history in such a way that his audience cannot determine whether the protagonist is the best or the worst of men, whether the central action springs from disinterested idealism or vainglorious egotism, whether that action is virtuous and necessary or wicked and gratuitous? Nor is one surprised to see that the most romantic and comic of Shakespeare's history plays was created at the moment when he was about to abandon romantic comedy, poised for flight into the greater tragedies with their profounder questions about the meaning of action and heroism. The clash between the two possible views of *Henry V* suggests a spiritual struggle in Shakespeare that he would spend the rest of his career working through. One sees a similar oscillation, magnified and reemphasized, in the problem plays and tragedies, and one is tempted to read the romances as a last profound effort to reconcile the irreconcilable. The terrible fact about *Henry V* is that Shakespeare seems equally tempted by both its rival gestalts. And he forces us, as we experience and reexperience and reflect on the play, as we encounter it in performances which inevitably lean in one direction or the other, to share his conflict.

Henry V is most valuable for us not because it points to a crisis in Shakespeare's spiritual life, but because it shows us something about ourselves: the simultaneity of our deepest hopes and fears about the world of political action. In this play, Shakespeare reveals the conflicts between the private selves with which we are born and the public selves we must become, between our longing that authority figures be like us and our suspicion that they must have traded away their inwardness for the sake of power. The play contrasts our hope that society can solve our problems with our knowledge that society has never done so. The inscrutability of *Henry V* is the in-scrutability of history. And for a unique moment in Shakespeare's work ambiguity is the heart of the matter, the single most important fact we must confront in plucking out the mystery of the world we live in.

"Alexander the Pig": Shakespeare on History and Poetry

David Quint

In one satirical scene of *Henry V*, Shakespeare criticizes a tradition of humanist ideas about the writing and reading of history. He specifically questions the assumption that the past possesses an inherently normative authority for the present, that the function of history is to produce exemplary models for human behavior. At the same time, he challenges the claim of the historian to provide a fully objective account of past events, uncolored by his own present circumstances and self-interest. The play thus denies to itself either of two canonical readings of the historical text: it presents itself neither as a collection of improving moral and political exemplars, nor as a true and impartial narration of historical fact.

Shakespeare's play thus finds a middle ground in the quarrel between humanism and historicism, a quarrel which was initiated in the self-reflections of Renaissance humanism and which has received its most distinguished modern contribution in the thought of Hans-Georg Gadamer. What Gadamer terms [in *Truth and Method*] the "effective-historical consciousness" (*wirkungsgeschichtliches Bewusstsein*) is constituted not only by an historicism that understands the temporal distance separating present from past, but also by a recognition that both past and present belong to the same continuum of historical tradition. This recognition, by which the present observer grasps the historical limitations—what Gadamer sees as a constantly shifting "horizon"—that contain and condition his own understanding, provides a common ground between present and past and is the basis for

From *boundary 2* 10, no. 3 (Spring 1982). © 1982 by *boundary 2*.

a dialogue between the two that is Gadamer's modified version of the hermeneutic circle. The undisguised ulterior motive of Gadamer's philosophical project is a saving of the past and its "classic" tradition: these remain an inexhaustible source of self-understanding for the present interpreter, even after a historicist critique has deprived them of any normative exemplarity. For Gadamer, this critique is a *fait accompli* of nineteenth-century intellectual history, and his own latter-day humanism is a reaction against an historicism which aims to acquire an objective, scientific mastery over the past; this mastery would isolate the past from the subjective experience of the present interpreter and rule out any exchange between them. The quarrel between humanism and historicism thus operates between, at one pole, the present's uncritical acceptance of the authority of the past, and, at the other, an equally uncritical investment of the present with authority over the past. These two positions also define the historical progress of the quarrel which arose when Renaissance humanists began to recognize the anachronism inherent in their attempts to imitate and relive the classical past and which has reopened to counter the triumph of historicism and of a modernism that announces its own definitive break with past tradition.

Shakespeare's criticism of historiography belongs to this quarrel's early stages. For most Renaissance humanists, the past retained the status of a classic; history was to be read as an exemplary text, a series of models held up for imitation. But the humanist cultural program was subject to self-criticism, produced by a nascent historicism that at once challenged the authority of the past and initiated a dialogue with it. The reflections of *Henry V* upon its own presentation of history allude to and grow out of this humanist self-criticism. The play, moreover, suggests how the rhetorical self-consciousness peculiar to the literary text could provide a model for a historical consciousness that succeeds in placing itself at a critical distance from the past. Whereas both ancient and humanist thought had defined the proper writing and reading of history in opposition to poetry—the latter conceived as an inauthentic rhetoric of persuasion—Shakespeare insistently points to the poetic components of his history-play and implies that such rhetorical structures inevitably shape the historical understanding. This literary mediation which reveals its own workings effectively separates the present from the past which it represents, and contributes to a sense of the past's otherness. At the same time the transformation of history into a nonauthoritative literary discourse allows the present interpreter to form a subjective critical response to the past rather than to find himself mastered by the force of historical example. In Shakespeare's poetic treatment, history ceases to be the didactic instrument of classical humanism and becomes instead an occasion for historical self-reflection.

The co-captains of the all-British Isles team which King Henry fields at Agincourt include the Welshman Fluellen, the Scot Jamy, the Irishman Macmorris, and the Englishman Gower. This collection of nationalities underscores the patriotic theme of *Henry V,* and provides intermittent comic relief from the battle carnage in the form of ethnic humor. One of the play's running jokes is Fluellen's inability to pronounce the letter B. The joke, it turns out, is to be taken seriously.

In act 4, scene 7, Fluellen and Gower express their somewhat mistaken appreciation of Henry's gallantry. At the end of the preceding scene, the king has ordered all the French prisoners killed, thereby operating "expressly against the law of arms." Henry's action comes not, as his two captains believe, in reprisal for the massacre of the English boys and baggage carriers, but rather as a tactical ploy in the face of a new French offensive. The pedant-soldier Fluellen tries to discover a resemblance between Henry and the outstanding military commander of antiquity.

FLU: Ay, he was porn at Monmouth, Captain Gower. What call you the town's name where Alexander the Pig was porn?

GOW: Alexander the Great.

FLU: Why, I pray you, is not pig great? the pig, or the great, or the mighty, or the huge, or the magnanimous, are all one reckonings, save the phrase is a little variations.

GOW: I think Alexander the Great was born in Macedon: his father was called Philip of Macedon, as I take it.

FLU: I think it is in Macedon where Alexander is porn. I tell you, captain, if you look in the maps of the 'orld, I warrant you sall find, in the comparisons between Macedon and Monmouth, that the situations, look you, is both alike. There is a river in Macedon, and there is also moreover a river in

> Monmouth: it is called Wye at Monmouth; but it is
> out of my prains what is the name of the other
> river; but 'tis all one, 'tis alike as my fingers is to
> my fingers, and there is salmons in both. If you
> mark Alexander's life well, Harry of Monmouth's
> life is come after it indifferent well; for there is fig-
> ures in all things. Alexander, God knows, and you
> know, in his rages, and his furies, and his wraths,
> and his cholers, and his moods, and his
> displeasures, and his indignations, and also being a
> little intoxicates in his prains, did, in his ales and his
> angers, look you, kill his best friend, Cleitus.
>
> GOW: Our king is not like him in that; he never killed
> any of his friends.
>
> FLU: It is not well done, mark you now, to take the tales
> out of my mouth, ere it is made and finished. I
> speak but in the figures and comparisons of it: as
> Alexander killed his friend Cleitus, being in his ales
> and his cups, so also Harry Monmouth, being in his
> right wits and his good judgments, turned away the
> fat knight with the great-belly doublet: he was full
> of jests, and gipes, and knaveries, and mocks; I
> have forgot his name.
>
> GOW: Sir John Falstaff.
>
> (4.7.12–53)

Whatever Henry might make of Fluellen's comparison, he is in no position to complain, having himself invoked the example of Alexander to exhort his troops once more into the breach of Harfleur (3.1.19). The allusion to Alexander's murder of Cleitus focuses attention upon the character who is never onstage: despite Gower's disclaimer and Fluellen's eventual twisting of his "figure" to transform Alexander into Henry's opposite, their exchange may second the opinion of the hostess that the king has killed Falstaff's heart (2.1.91) or, as Nym puts it, "The King hath run bad humors on the knight" (1.3.124). Alive or dead, Falstaff haunts the play from the wings. Shakespeare intensifies rather than alleviates the feelings of uneasiness about Henry's character aroused by the rejection of the fat old knight at the end of *Henry IV, Part 2*.

    The story of Alexander the Great and Cleitus was familiar to

Renaissance schoolboys in the Latin *History of Alexander* of Quintus Curtius, a work translated into English by J. Brend in 1553. In Curtius's dramatic account of the incident, Alexander, swelled with wine and pride in his conquests, belittles the achievements of his father, Philip of Macedon. Irritated by the boastfulness of the younger generation at the expense of the Macedonian veterans, Cleitus, one of Philip's officers, counters with a verse of Euripides to the effect that kings steal away the glory won by the blood of others. He further mocks Alexander's pretensions to be the son not of Philip, but of Jupiter Ammon. Enraged, the young king seizes a spear and runs his trusted lieutenant through. But Alexander is immediately filled with remorse, remembering that the same Cleitus had once saved his life.

This classical instance of unbridled violence, loaded with parricidal overtones, corresponds to Nym's earlier assessment of the Henry who rejects the false father, Falstaff. Nym asserts:

> The king is a good king: but it must be as it may; he
> passes some humors, and careers.
>
> (2.1.128–29)

But Fluellen is quick to explain that Henry is precisely not a violently "humorous" or capricious ruler: he is the sober king who banishes drunken vice from his court. In fact, Gower and Fluellen have reversed themselves. They began by praising Henry for being anything but cool-headed—for slitting the throats of the French prisoners out of revenge. The audience, however, knows that Henry actually acted from policy, the "good judgments" which the two captains attribute to the banishment of Falstaff. Yet, at the end of the captain's colloquy, Henry himself appears, fresh from the heat of battle.

> I was not angry since I came to France
> Until this instant.
>
> (4.7.57–58)

The king now seems to be out for blood, and he repeats his order to kill the prisoners. The Shakespearean complexity not only makes a puzzle out of Henry's motivation but also suggests that confusion of values in the minds of the captains who attempt to judge him. The question may be posed, however, whether it makes any difference to the slaughtered prisoners or to the dead Falstaff whether Henry acts out of anger or wise restraint. Fluellen insists that Henry is a second Alexander. But Alexander, after all, was a pig.

I. EXCURSUS: ALEXANDER, HISTORY, AND POETRY

Fluellen's classical exemplum refers the play's ambivalence towards Henry to a Renaissance debate over Alexander's moral character, a debate whose larger subject was the didactic usefulness of reading history. This debate was formulated in the humanist manuals on education written during the first four decades of the sixteenth century, and its terms had become commonplaces by the century's end. Humanist educators regarded Alexander's career as proof of the effectiveness of their pedagogical theories, which stressed the practical application of classroom learning to politics and the business of living. Alexander had been instructed by Aristotle, the greatest philosopher-teacher of his age, and the result was the conquest of the world and countless deeds of prowess and virtue. Beginning in the Italian *quattrocento,* anecdotes about Aristotle and Alexander crop up with regularity in humanist educational treatises, demonstrating the link between the liberal arts and political achievement. The damaging incident of Cleitus remained to be explained, but here the humanists turned to the testimony of Quintillian. Before employing Aristotle, Philip had placed Alexander under the tutelage of one Leonidas, a man of unspecified bad habits which were transmitted to the young prince. The effects of a vice inculcated in childhood surfaced many years later in the drunken banquet and murder of Cleitus. The negative example of Leonidas, an unaccountable human error in the formation of the future hero, only confirmed the humanist belief in the power of education, and underscored the need for parental vigilance in the choice of a proper teacher.

Alexander's curriculum under Aristotle resembled the one which the humanists proposed for their own pupils: he read the classics. The young prince's primary texts were the Homeric poems. Sir Thomas Elyot, in *The Book Named the Governor* (1531), uses the example of Alexander to demonstrate Homer's utility in the classroom.

> For in his books he contained and most perfectly expressed, not only the documents martial and discipline of arms, but also incomparable wisdom, and instructions for political governance of people, with the worthy commendation and

laud of noble princes; wherewith the readers shall be so all inflamed that they most fervently shall desire and covet, by the imitation of their virtues, to acquire semblance glory. For the which occasion, Aristotle, most sharp-witted and excellent learned philosopher, as soon as he had received Alexander from King Philip his father, he before any other thing taught him the most noble works of Homer; wherein Alexander found such sweetness and fruit that ever after he had Homer not only with him in all his journeys but also laid him under his pillow when he went to rest, and often times would purposely wake some hours of the night to take as it were his pastime with that most noble poet.

Homer's main lessons are political and military, the appropriate fare for the future magistrates and civil servants, towards whom, as his title suggests, Elyot directed his educational program. Elyot describes the imitation of literary models which lies at the core of nearly all humanist pedagogical method. The student is inspired to copy the example of the great men he encounters in his reading. Alexander particularly venerated Achilles, from whom he claimed descent.

This same method of study, with its emphasis on imitation, could be applied to historical writing. Elyot again has recourse to a classical precedent, Scipio Africanus, who was said to have learned the rules of good government and soldiership from Xenophon's didactic history of Cyrus. Similarly, Alexander's own life and deeds became a textbook for the Renaissance schoolboy. Included on Elyot's recommended reading list is

> Quintus Curtius, who writeth the life of King Alexander elegantly and sweetly. In whom may be found the figure of an excellent prince, as he that incomparably excelled all other kings and emperors in wisdom, hardiness, strength, policy, agility, valiant courage, nobility, liberality, and courtesy, wherein he was a spectacle or mark for all princes to look on. Contrariwise when he was once vanquished with volupty and pride his tyranny and beastly cruelty abhorreth all readers.

The misgivings about Alexander's later career, which includes the murder of Cleitus, are presented almost as a parenthetical afterthought. The Macedonian conqueror remains for Elyot a "spectacle," a mirror for magistrates-in-training in which all human virtues are reflected. Twenty-two separate appeals to Alexander's example are scattered through the pages of *The Governor*. Alexander enjoys a similar prominence in the *De l'Institution du Prince* (1540) of the French humanist Guillaume Budé, a work that is largely a collection of moralizing biographical anecdotes about the great men of antiquity. To judge from the space and number of anecdotes devoted to him, Alexander ranks second only to Pompey in Budé's estimation.

For his pedagogical purpose, Elyot recognizes little distinction between poetic fiction and historical fact. Both poetry and history are repositories of the edifying classical exemplum held up for modern imitation. Their twin status in the humanist literary education is suggested in a passage where Elyot announces a recent addition to the humanist curriculum.

> It would not be forgotten that the little book of the most excellent doctor Erasmus Roteradamus (which he wrote to Charles, now being Emperor and then Prince of Castile), which book is entitled *The Institution of a Christian Prince*, would be as familiar alway with gentleman at all times and in every age as was Homer with the great King Alexander, or Xenophon with Scipio.

While Alexander carried Homer with him throughout his campaigns, Scipio "was never seen without his book of Xenophon." If the notable results of these intensive reading courses were any indication—and there is little to choose between Alexander and Scipio in a contest of ancient virtues—the poet and the historian seemed to be equally effective counsellors and teachers to the schoolboy-leader.

Erasmus's *Institutio Principis Christiani* was published in 1516. Elyot's enthusiastic recommendation is somewhat peculiar, since the Erasmian treatise constitutes a radical revision of those pedagogical premises which the continental Renaissance inherited from Italian humanism, premises which still inform the thought of the *Governor*. Erasmus's new outlook can be detected from the very beginning of the *Institutio,* in his dedicatory epistle to Charles which contains an extended comparison of the future emperor to his ancient counterpart, Alexander.

> But as much as you surpass Alexander in good fortune, mighty prince Charles, so much do we hope you will sur-

pass him in wisdom. For he had gained a mighty empire, albeit one not destined to endure, solely through blood-shed. You have been born to a splendid kingdom and are destined to a still greater one. As Alexander had to toil to carry out his invasions, so will you have to labor to yield, rather than to gain, part of your power. You owe it to the powers of the heaven that you came into a kingdom unstained with blood, bought through no evil connection. It will be the lot of your wisdom to keep it bloodless and peaceful.

The sentiment that Charles may surpass the achievements of Alexander goes beyond the usual flattery to princes that precedes most Renaissance books. Erasmus intends to found the ethical basis of humanist education in religion, a plan which does not so much alter the basic method of imitation as the subject matter to be imitated. The Christian king described in the title of his treatise and outlined in its pages is a pacifist in principle who has no use for the ancient military heroes. His proper model, as for all Christians, is the example of Christ in the gospels.

> Now what could be more senseless than for a man who has received the sacraments of the Christian church to set up as an example for himself Alexander, Julius Caesar, or Xerxes, for even the pagan writers would have attacked their lives if any of them had had a little sounder judgment?

This opinion is echoed by Rabelais in the person of old King Grandgousier in the *Gargantua*.

> Le temps n'est plus d'ainsi conquester les royaulmes avecques dommaige de son prochain frere christian. Ceste imitation des anciens Hercules, Alexandres, Hannibalz, Scipions, Cesars, et aultres telz, est contraire à la profession de l'Evangile.

Reading and emulating the classics may indeed produce a negative effect, feeding the dreams of military glory which Rabelais satirizes in Picrochole, whom his counsellors promise to make "le plus heureux, le plus chevalureux prince qui oncques feut depuis la mort de Alexandre Macedon." In his *De Causis Corruptarum Artium* (1531), the Spanish Erasmian Juan Luis Vives sees a direct literary link in the murderous chain of historical events.

> The name of Achilles incited Alexander, Alexander Caesar, Caesar many others; Caesar killed in his various battles 192,000 men, not counting the civil wars.

For Vives, each despot imitates and tries to outdo the predecessor about whom he reads. This kind of classical education leads to more and more bloodshed. Among his other efforts to emulate Achilles, Alexander ordered the heels of his valiant captive Betis to be pierced, and then dragged him behind his chariot as Homer's hero had treated the body of Hector. Montaigne gives prominence to this story by recounting it in the first of his *Essais*.

Vives couples Achilles and Alexander as negative models, assuming that both poetry and history are read in order to be imitated. The failure of the humanist literary education to define different reader's responses to fiction and nonfiction will create the dilemma of Don Quixote who imitates the outlandish heroes of chivalry *as if* they were historical figures. The possibility of such a confusion of poetry and history may account for the mistrust of imaginative literature which occasionally surfaces in humanist thought. In the *De Corruptio,* Vives inveighs precisely against the "Spanish Amadis and Florisand, Lancelot and the French round table, and the Italian Roland," quixotic books of pure fable which corrupt their readers "not otherwise than those of delicate stomach, who are the most indulged, and who are sustained by sugary and honeyed condiments, spitting out any solid food." Vives disjoins the traditional Lucretian metaphor of the sugar-coated pill, the combination of the *dulce,* the pleasurable, and the *utile,* the useful, the metaphor which Tasso would use to justify his inclusion of Roland-like chivalric fictions into his historical epic of the First Crusade. Vives insists upon the necessity of keeping history and poetry apart. When historians mix lies with facts, they are following the example of poets who,

> because they strove after only the pleasure of their hearers and, as it were, the tickling of their ears, only pursued those things which give pleasure; and because occasionally they did not trust to succeed with the real truth of things, they both mixed false things with true ones, and distorted that same truth in the direction where they thought it

would have more grace and admiration: they abused to that end figures of speech, metaphors, allegories, ambiguities, analogies between things and between names.

Vives's remarks occur in the context of a discussion of historiography. In spite of his rejection of history as a subject for imitation, he rehearses a series of classical criticisms that formed the standard humanist rules for good history-writing. These almost all derive from the treatise, *How to Write History,* by the second century A.D. Greek satirist, Lucian of Samosata. Translated into Latin by Pirckheimer in 1515, the work was the most influential and widely read ancient theoretical discussion of history in the Renaissance. Lucian succinctly spells out the problem of the pleasurable and the useful.

> Now some think they can make a satisfactory distinction in history between what gives pleasure and what is useful, and for this reason work eulogy into it as giving pleasure and enjoyment to its readers; but do you see how far they are from the truth? In the first place, the distinction they draw is false: history has one task and one end—what is useful—and that comes from truth alone.

Lucian decries the practice among his contemporary historians to eulogize the often less-than-great men whose deeds they record. Their methods include formal panegyric and the inclusion of mythological episodes: "But if history introduces flattery of that sort, what else does it become but a sort of prose poetry. . . ?" Vives similarly accuses certain Greek historians of performing the Lucianic rhetorical trick of turning a gnat into an Indian elephant by so extolling a mediocre man that "if you consider with what praise they adorn him, you would expect to be reading about someone more outstanding than Alexander, Caesar, or Pompey." Vives further notes the patriotic biases of contemporary historians who expand upon the glories and conceal the faults of their particular nations: "The fools do not realize that this is not writing history, but taking up the cause of that nation, which is the way of an advocate, not of a historian."

Despite his insistence upon the separation of history and poetry, Lucian does not deny a kind of artistry to historical style. He describes the task of the historian to give a fine arrangement to events and illuminate them as vividly as possible. And when a man who has heard him thinks thereafter that he is actually seeing what is being described and then praises him—then it is that the work of our Phidias of history is perfect and has received its proper praise.

The aim of writing history is to make the truth appear true. Lucian compares the ideal history to the lifelike sculpture of Phidias. The historian's craft produces a heightened verisimilitude which causes the reader to forget the literary medium of the text. The ability to make the narrated events seem to take place before the reader's eyes is the source of the power of the historical text—a power which may be abused. Guillaume Budé echoes Lucian's precepts with a warning.

Car la nature de l'Histoire n'est aultre chose, que suiure la pure verité des faicts, & les reciter de telle sorte, qu'il semble qu'ilz se facent plus tost lors qu'on les list, que qu'ilz soient escripts. Aultrement, si on n'observoit la verité: l'Histoire se deueroit nommer une honteuse fable, & non pas estre honorée d'vn si honneste tiltre, que lon doibt tenir aussy certain, que la certitude propre.

Truth is absolutely essential to a history whose style aims to persuade the reader of the factuality of the deeds it depicts. Lucian dwells upon the need for impartiality and independence, enjoining the prospective historian to tell the truth no matter whom it pleases or displeases. He cites specific examples.

He must not be concerned that Philip has had his eye put out by Aster of Amphipolis, the archer at Olynthus—he must show him exactly as he was. Nor must he mind if Alexander is going to be angry when he gives a clear account of the cruel murder of Cleitus at the banquet.

The murder of Cleitus, the bloody stain upon Alexander's glorious career, is a classical test case for objectivity in historical writing.

But it is precisely the historian's refusal to prettify his subject matter with a flattery which Lucian equates with poetry that makes history unacceptable for the humanist schools of Erasmus and Vives. The dilemma in which their advocacy of historical impartiality placed the humanist teachers who sought to instruct through literary models could be viewed in terms of a contradictory understanding of the relationship of history to poetry: history was to be *read* in the same way as poetry but *written* in opposition to poetic norms. Sir Philip Sidney seizes upon this contradiction in his *Apology for Poetry* (1595) in order to demonstrate the didactic superiority of poetry to history. Sidney follows a long line of sixteenth-century Italian critics who rediscovered in Aristotle's *Poetics* the dictum that poetry is more philosophical than history because the poet deals with universals while the historian is confined to particular events: poetry shows man as he should be, not as he too often is. This critical tradition asserted that Xenophon's idealized portrait of Cyrus in the *Cyropaedia* is not—as Elyot had maintained—history at all, but a kind of poetry. But this poetic heightening of the pages of history, according to Sidney, redeems history for the classroom.

> But if the question be for your own use and learning, whether it be better to have it set down as it should be or as it was, then certainly is more doctrinable the feigned Cyrus in Xenophon than the true Cyrus in Justin, and the feigned Aeneas in Virgil than the right Aeneas in Dares Phrygius.

Sidney defends the poetic supplements to history which Vives, following Lucian, had condemned. Rather than keeping poetry and history apart, Sidney claims that poetic embellishment will produce a more "doctrinable" textbook out of history. By contrast, the historian who must stick to the facts can only present an ambivalent portrait of human behavior.

> the historian, bound to tell things as things were, cannot be liberal (without he will be poetical) of a perfect pattern, but as in Alexander or Scipio himself, show doings, some to be liked, some to be misliked. And then how will you discern what to follow but by your own discretion, which you had without reading Quintus Curtius?

Sidney adapts his Aristotelian defense of poetry to the pedagogical concerns shared by the humanist educators, and his argument exploits the division in their thought which followed the Erasmian rejection of secular history from the moral curriculum. As the example of Alexander attests, history mixes depictions of virtue and vice and provides no absolute model for the student to follow. The absolute model that the Erasmians found in the imitation of Christ Sidney posits in the "perfect pattern" of the poetic hero.

II. SHAKESPEARE, THE POET-HISTORIAN

Fluellen would obviously prefer a perfect Henry to the ambiguous Alexander. The Welshman "poetizes" history, displaying all the vices which Lucianic advocates of impartial, factual historiography most deplore: he abuses analogy, he devotes himself to panegyric, he is guided by nationalistic prejudice, he inflates his king into another Alexander. But this same rhetoric betrays him. Adducing the salmons and rivers of Monmouth and Macedon, Fluellen's argument for the similarity of Henry and Alexander is preposterously weak, but Henry does indeed begin to look like Alexander precisely at the moment when Fluellen reverses himself and protests their dissimilarity. Fluellen can neither persuade the audience that Henry resembles Alexander *in bono* nor that Henry does *not* resemble Alexander *in malo,* the murderer of Cleitus. The result is not a poetically embellished portrait of the perfect prince, but rather the complicated, morally indeterminate Henry of Shakespeare's play. By satirizing Fluellen's inept use of the encomiastic style, the play portrays a poetic temptation to the historian to which it apparently knows better than to succumb. Furthermore, at the moment when Henry has committed his one unmitigatedly blameworthy deed—the killing of the French prisoners—the play refers to Alexander's murder of Cleitus, the retelling of which, according to Lucian, exemplified the need for objective history. Showing Henry's action as it was, rather than joining Fluellen and Gower in trying to find justification and praise for it, the play seems to come down squarely on the side of the historian against the poet.

Fluellen is neither the play's worst nor most ludicrous offender in the practice of panegyric flattery. That distinction must belong to the French Dauphin who writes sonnets on the glories of his horse (3.7). Renaissance readers knew that the ancients had set for themselves the rhetorical exercise of composing eulogies in praise of trivial subjects—salt, gnats, and the like—and Erasmus's revival of the custom produced one of the comic masterpieces of their age. The Dauphin, however, seems to be quite literal about his horse.

> it is a theme as fluent as the sea; turn the sands into elo-
> quent tongues, and my horse is argument for them all.
> (3.7.34–37)

The inexhaustible subject requires a comparable eloquence and the Dauphin's equine encomium seems to call for a comic version of the rhetorical *copia* which Erasmus and his fellow humanist educators sought to inculcate in their pupils. The ideal orator should not only have something to say on an infinite number of subjects, but be able to speak on any one subject in an infinite number of ways. The eulogizing Fluellen seems to have a special predilection for this rhetorical method ("his rages, and his furies, and his wraths, and his cholers, and his moods, and his displeasures, and his indignations," "jests, and gipes, and knaveries, and mocks"). He appeals to *copia* to defend his substitution of "Alexander the Pig" for "Alexander the Great."

> Why, I pray you, is not pig great? the pig, or the great, or
> the mighty, or the huge, or the magnanimous, are all one
> reckonings, save the phrase is a little variations.

By "little" variation, "great" becomes "big," which becomes "pig." Here, too, Fluellen's language comically backfires, and his attempt to improve his subject with rhetorical elegance merely introduces ambiguity, not only about Alexander and Henry, but about all the other great, mighty, huge and magnanimous.

The joke, however, works two ways. The bungling Fluellen satirizes the poetizers of history, but Fluellen is himself a poetic character with no historical existence outside the fiction of the play. His difficulty with the letter B is a poetic choice—the more so since Fluellen pronounces his Bs correctly on occasion (between, but, being). There is a providence in the slip of the tongue, the providence of the playwright who here asserts his control over the script. When Fluellen Welshes "big" into "pig," the play sends up his version of history only to fall back upon its own: where the minimal phonemic difference between two labial consonants attests to the inability of "historical meaning" to be independent of the language through which it is transmitted. No less than the playwright, the writer of history has the last word because he uses words—which are not interchangeable parts of an ornamental whole, "all one reckonings," as the copious rhetorician Fluellen appears to think, but which rather fragment the empirical historical event into a series of discrete descriptive possibilities from which the historian chooses his authorized version.

The disclosure of an authorial presence violates one of the stylistic canons of Renaissance historiography. The verisimilar style defined by Lucian, which aims to make the reader an eyewitness to the historical event, suppresses the literary mediation of the historian to the point where his own narrative voice virtually disappears. Sir Thomas North's translation (1579) of Jacques Amyot's preface to his French translation of Plutarch's *Lives* (1559) commends this "lively" style for allowing the reader a full if vicarious identification with its historical subject matter.

> as in the very reading of them we see our minds to be so touched by them, not as though the things were already done and past, but as though they were even then presently in doing, and we find ourselves carried away with gladness and grief through fear or hope, well near as though we were then at the doing of them.

There is an implicit link between the verisimilitude which almost makes the reader a participant in the event itself, and the truth and objectivity of the historian; for Budé, the style does not merely reflect but also enjoins the writer's impartiality. By pointing through Fluellen to its own playwright-historian and breaching the verisimilar style, Shakespeare's play criticizes such stylistic assumptions. This criticism reverses the relationship of style and content, suggesting that the historian's verisimilitude *creates the appearance* of his impartiality, thereby reducing historical objectivity to a trick of style, a rhetorical trope. Whereas the clumsy rhetorician Fluellen lets his biases show and cannot convince the audience of a word he says, the considerably adroit Shakespeare may be more persuasive. The audience may accept the play's truthlike version of history as historical truth unless the playwright steps forward to call his representation into question.

Instead, Shakespeare sends the magniloquent Chorus of *Henry V* onstage. Appearing before each act and as an epilogue, the Chorus ostensibly seeks to create or enhance the verisimilitude of the performance. The spectator is asked to suspend disbelief and supplement the stage business with his imagination. But the Chorus simultaneously criticizes the play's lack of verisimilitude—otherwise

his own function would be superfluous. He laments the inadequacy
of theatrical representation for the great subject at hand.

> But pardon, gentles all,
> The flat unraised spirits that hath dar'd
> On this unworthy scaffold to bring forth
> So great an object: can this cockpit hold
> The vasty fields of France? or may we cram
> Within this wooden O the very casques
> That did affright the air at Agincourt?
> (prologue, 8–14)

> There is the playhouse now, there must you sit;
> And thence to France shall we convey you safe
> And bring you back, charming the narrow seas
> To give you gentle pass; for, if we may,
> We'll not offend one stomach with our play.
> (act 2 prologue, 36–40)

> And so our scene must to the battle fly;
> Where, O for pity! we shall much disgrace
> With four or five most vile and ragged foils,
> Right ill-dispos'd in brawl ridiculous,
> The name of Agincourt. Yet sit and see;
> Minding true thing by what their mock'ries be.
> (act 4 prologue, 48–53)

The theatrical illusion which the Chorus seems to promote with one
hand—the illusion of verisimilitude which might lead the spectator
to take the actions of the play for the "true things" of history—he
apologetically dispels with the other, showing those actions up as
"mock'ries." The Chorus exposes the actors, scene changes, and
stage properties for what they are as well as for what they represent.
The imperfect verisimilitude he describes preserves rather than reduces the distance between the audience and the play, a distance
spelled out in spatial terms by the conceit of the playhouse as a
ferryboat crossing and recrossing the Channel to follow the action on
its stage.

Shakespeare frequently finds devices to distance the spectator
from the stage action of his plays. In the discourse of *Henry V*, the
willed aesthetic distance—maintained both inside the action by
Fluellen's unintentionally comic history-within-a-history and out-

side the action by the speeches of the Chorus—corresponds to a recognition of *historical distance*. Dramatizing rather than concealing the hybrid nature of his play which is both history and poetry, Shakespeare points to the literary mediation separating the audience from the historical event. The play's focus upon the literary act which re-creates the event both denies to history-writing its aura of unmediated and empirical truth and suggests that the truth about the event may be ultimately irrecoverable across the gap of time. This skepticism is underscored thematically by the play's confusing, contradictory portrait of Henry. If even the eyewitnesses Gower and Fluellen cannot discern the motivation of their king, who is now one thing, now another, how can the historian-poet who was not present at Agincourt?

No less than the indecision about Henry which deprives the play of a clear-cut model prince, the perception of historical distance inhibits imitation, the stock didactic response to history advocated in humanist educational theory. Imitation would collapse the distance between the reader-playgoer and the historical event. So would the historical analogy: if, as Fluellen claims, "there is figures in all things," the identity found between events blurs their historical specificity. The anachronism of imitation and analogy finds literary expression in the verisimilar style, and it is thus not surprising to find the same humanists who recommend the imitation of historical models also upholding an historical style which creates the illusion of simultaneity between the act of reading and the events which that style narrates. The preservation of distance in Shakespeare's play allows a critical response to the historical event which perceives its otherness from the experience of the present interpreter. The recognition of the difference between past and present pulls apart historical analogies and questions the validity of finding norms for human behavior in the actions of the past. The distanced interpreter of *Henry V* must judge its action for himself, and the play demands from him an act of self-reflection just as it reflects upon its own act of writing and interpreting history.

It may seem paradoxical that Shakespeare should demonstrate an historicist understanding of the past by turning it into a poetic text. But it is possible that Renaissance thought could more easily recognize the historical otherness of texts than of events. The humanist revolution in historical thought originated in the discipline of philology which developed critical principles for the reading of texts.

This reading, to be sure, was put in the service of a rhetorical program and applied to practical affairs. But the twin aims of humanism, supposed to be complementary, proved contradictory. By placing the text in a given historical context, philology calls into question its applicability to the present rhetorical moment. This is essentially the same contradiction explored in Shakespeare's play, which replaces the historical event with a literary text of which the event is only one of several constituent parts that philology can break down and analyze. Such analysis discovers that historical meaning does not consist in a series of prescriptive models which the past may hand down and impose upon a passive present age, but is rather the product of an active process of interpretation by which the present may also define itself in relationship to the past. A critical understanding of the past may thus have first emerged through the recognition of the historical text as text. This critical understanding, with its unsettling effects upon a humanism which rests upon tradition and imitation, lies at the basis of Shakespeare's historical enterprise.

The "Image Bound":
Icon and Iconoclasm in *Henry V*

James R. Siemon

The notion of Shakespearean art as a series of varied, but related, "images" of internal conceptual unities would seem easiest to demonstrate in such works as the narrative poem *The Rape of Lucrece* or in the partially narrated history play *Henry V*. Both poem and play are patterned by obvious controlling metaphors: in *Lucrece* the visual image of Troy's betrayal and violation repeats the tragedy of the protagonist, while in *Henry V* the verbal image of the bee's commonwealth clearly images the play's history of contrary wills brought to one purpose. Besides their use of narrative commentary and their obvious patterning, features both works share with standard allegory, the two also employ emblematic staging—whether physical or, in the case of the poem, imagined—to establish abstract meanings for characters and their actions. Furthermore, since the integrity of this underlying meaning depends on the poet's modification of pre-existing story or history, the two works offer useful examples of those imaginative techniques for the making of many into one that Coleridge found so Shakespearean, and that his disciples, the imagery critics, have continued to find important.

At the same time, however, the two works also exhibit incongruities in their very manifestations of unity, and they thereby suggest troubles to come in the later works. In *Lucrece* disunity is more suggested than realized, appearing as lines of stress in an otherwise dominant coherence. In *Henry V* the flaws are more insistent, like the

From *Shakespearean Iconoclasm.* © 1985 by the Regents of the University of California. University of California Press, 1985.

wretches in Henry's prison managing to make their existence felt even as the play seems bent on directing attention to the "Mirror of all Christian Kings" and, through him, to the noble virtues for which he is the "pattern" or living icon. Coming when it does, in the period just preceding the composition of the great tragedies, *Henry V* serves as a warning far more troubling than the confusions and difficulties of earlier plays such as *Titus Andronicus;* for in the case of *Henry V,* we encounter a drama that seems conscious, even deliberate in its employment of incongruity and dissonance. . . .

Henry V comes close to realizing the values of Lucrece's painting in the medium of poetic drama. There are moments when the play forms iconic tableaux that seem quite as significant as does the painting of Troy to the work in which it occurs. Yet the meaningful stasis into which the play often appears to settle is repeatedly disrupted by an iconoclastic counterforce which demands that one notice the particulars—the how, why, by whom, and of what substance—such moments are made.

The play comes closest to being iconic in its treatment of Henry himself. Repeatedly the "mirror of all Christian kings" (a model as essentially defined as is Hecuba for "all" sorrow) is caught in appropriately stylized postures—in council, at wooing, in the field, and so forth. A procession of such ideal images is clearly what the prologue envisions for proper tribute to Henry:

> Then should the warlike Harry, like himself,
> Assume the port of Mars; and at his heels,
> Leash'd in like hounds, should famine, sword, and fire
> Crouch for employment.
>
> (ll. 5–8)

And to the end of rendering Henry both as this icon of Mars and as the mirror of martial kingship, the play takes certain definite steps in its attempt to make him appear as much "like himself" as possible. (This is the emblem of war in *A Mirror for Magistrates*.)

One of these iconizing strategies is the play's violent abbreviation of historical time. Action that took place during the six-year period from Lent of 1414 to May 1420 is greatly compressed, while the various French dauphins of the period are condensed into the single figure of "the Dauphin." Beyond these condensations of time and character, certain cause and effect relationships are radically altered as well. So, for example, all references to the battles fought after Henry's return to France in 1417 are eliminated, creating the impression that the English victory at Agincourt was the direct cause of the French readiness to make peace. Furthermore, certain specific actions are strategically altered in order to draw attention away from their true origins and direct it instead to a focus on the present moment.

These strategies—abbreviating time, condensing character, and diverting attention from causal and genetic relationships—play their part in rendering Henry as an icon. The shortening of historical time frees Henry's image from a welter of distracting (if not unflattering) detail. The condensation of dauphins heightens the sense of simple opposition suggested by the Chorus's vision of "two mighty monarchies" confronting one another. And the elision of cause and genesis works to create strong impressions of Henry's virtuous effectiveness. From these processes there might well emerge an image of Christian kingship as compelling as that of Hecuba as a model of hopeless sorrow; but unlike the painted icon of all grief, the dramatic icon of militant English Christianity is seriously challenged by the work of art in which it is set. For every moment in which the play seems to be providing clear graphic embodiment of praiseworthy virtues, there are problems. In fact, the dramatic world of *Henry V* is haunted by the archbishop of Canterbury's pronouncement of the Protestant doctrine of the cessation of miracles:

> miracles are ceas'd:
> And therefore we must needs admit the means
> How things are perfected.
>
> (1.1.67–69)

The difference between this "means" of things and what they may be said to "mean" in themselves is crucial to an understanding of the play's complex operations. For one example of this difference, in the case of Henry's act of forgiving the drunken railer, the action (which is Shakespeare's invention from first to last) signifies his royal Christian magnanimity—if, that is, the moment is considered by itself, quite apart from the larger context in which it arises. The dramatic sight of Henry iconically embodying this quality tempts one to forget the role otherwise played by this moment as part of Henry's ongoing conflict with the rebels, and it is precisely this restricted interpretation that Laurence Olivier gives to the incident in his film of the play. With strategic editing, Olivier manages to represent Henry's act of forgiveness as an image signifying *only* magnanimity. Such a use of the image precisely parallels that analyzed by Roland Barthes in his discussion of a magazine photo of an African in French uniform saluting the French flag. As Barthes says, the powerful clarity of the image encourages the viewer to forget both the complicated history surrounding its origins and the designs implicit in its ends, suggesting instead that one simply accept its meaning as given, or "natural" (*Mythologies*). As the "natural" position of the African is supposed to be obeisance to the self-evident glories of European civilization, so the English who reject Henry are meant to be thought unnatural "monsters" (2.2.85), whose actions are "inhuman" (l. 95), cruel beyond all "natural cause" (l. 107). After all, Henry's natural generosity has just been demonstrated, and it is to this very quality in him that the conspirators themselves will appeal when revealed in their deceit.

To take this incident as it seems to be asking to be taken obviously calls for ignorance both of its genesis in Henry's own schemes against the rebels and of the historical sequence lying behind their rebellion. Surprisingly, however, this very scene reminds one of both, recalling the struggles of Henry's father and mentioning Henry's plots to apprehend the traitors in public view. One is pointedly reminded of the means, the why and how behind the scene, even when such spurs to consciousness severely complicate its import through their contradiction of an otherwise clear-cut meaning. Thus the play breaks out of the circumscribed limits of allegory (Henry's actions = magnanimity) and pushes instead into something resembling the realm of history, where, at each moment, disorder and discrepancy force one to take up the burden of interpretation, to consider before and after, origin and end, purpose and conclusion, without any promise of satisfying certainty to come. In sum, *Henry V* seems to want things in the way both of Lucrece and of Tarquin. All those pleas from the Chorus, beseeching the audience to work thoughts or grapple minds to the story, to follow, bless, and believe in Henry, are asking for a Lucretian reaction to the image; while time and again the play provides disturbing details, odd resonances, that seem to call out for a Tarquinian reaction instead.

Examples are everywhere. On one hand, there is Henry in the first act, the very image of long-suffering righteousness provoked to wrath, raising his "rightful hand in a well-hallowed cause" (1.2.293). But, on the other hand, the play demonstrates that the king's clerical advisers are anything but disinterested in their detailing of his infringed "right." Their testimony is explicitly shown to originate in a desire for political protection and so cannot but appear as a calculated attempt to tell Henry what he wants to hear. (Shakespeare even goes so far as to suggest, surely ironically, the many quite proper and Christian uses, both civil and military, to which this wealth might otherwise be put [1.1.11–19]. In the *Famous Victories of Henry V* [London, 1598] the whole speech detailing Henry's right consists of four lines.) The evidence of underlying political/historical means by which Henry's claim arises severely undercuts the meaning conveyed by his posture of righteous indignation. It may be true, as Bullough has pointed out, that there is no source for Shakespeare's portrayal of the "dignity of Henry's answer, his insistence on his kingly state . . . his majesty, and his appeal to the will of God." And it is undeniable that the playwright has carefully and unhistorically placed the incident of the tennis balls so that Henry's kingly rage might have some appearance of justification in heated blood. Yet, as the Chorus has suggested, the value of a cipher is inseparable from its position in the series that extends before and after it; and the same rule holds true for this compromised image of kingly resolution. Preceded by Henry's decision to bend France to his will or "break it all to pieces" (1.2.225) and followed by the troubling disproportionality between the Dauphin's "mock" and Henry's threat to mock widows, mothers, cities, and generations yet unborn out of life and limb (ll. 282–96), the stance of righteousness appears as hollow as an empty cipher.

As another example of the conflict between iconic and iconoclastic impulses in the play, the siege of Harfleur is striking. In preparing the audience to witness the siege, the Chorus promises a scene of truly epic martial achievement. Like mighty cannon, the puissant English "cavaliers" will bear down "all before them." And Henry's two lengthy speeches do, in fact, create the impression that he commands great powers—both literally in the form of troops and figuratively in the rhetorical facility that wins the French surrender. In these scenes, the play would seem to be presenting in compact, emblematic form Henry's powers of leadership and oratory. But this image does not fit so well when seen in the contexts that the play provides.

Henry's fiery exhortation, which urges the English peers to live up to their noble ancestry and the yeomen to make good on the equally noble promise glowing in their own eyes (3.1.17–30), although it certainly creates a compelling image of properly regal oratory, rings hollow when followed by a view of the men in the field. Instead of noble luster, one finds the lesser lights of Macmorris's blind fury ("I would have blowed up the town, so Chrish save me, la! in an hour") and of Bardolph, Nym, and Pistol's cowardice. Indeed, it is not the force of oratory but of blows that sends these last as close as they come to doing battle, as Fluellen drives them toward the action. This crew scarcely bear all before them, and, by the same token, Harfleur does not exactly fling wide its gates in response to Henry's just argument and in full confidence of his mercy. Through the juxtaposition of his speech with the surrender of the town (3.3), it might seem that the speech is the cause of the surrender. But the governor reveals that, in fact, his capitulation is rather a response to the Dauphin's decision to abandon the town:

> Our expectation hath this day an end.
> The Dauphin, whom of succors we entreated,
> Returns us that his powers are yet not ready
> To raise so great a siege. Therefore, great king,
> We yield our town and lives to thy soft mercy.
> (3.3.44–48)

Still, all this is not to say that Henry's speech is uninteresting; on the contrary, whatever its relationship to the surrender of Harfleur, it does occasion some interesting problems.

For instance, how ought one take the language of Henry's threats?

> Your naked infants spitted upon pikes,
> Whiles the mad mothers with their howls confus'd
> Do break the clouds, as did the wives of Jewry
> At Herod's bloody-hunting slaughtermen.
> (3.3.38–41)

With these lines, the positive image, which seems to be the purpose of this episode as a whole, suffers grotesque disfigurement. It is not the threat of cruelty that makes these lines so troubling either. After all, cruel words may serve in the present situation as substitutes for crueler deeds undone. The problem is instead the way Henry's speech has suddenly recast the virtue of *kingly oratory* that is otherwise exemplified by this scene into its negative form as *tyrannical rant*. Henry the Christian orator and king has become, in his own figures, Herod the ranting tyrant. This, of course, is exactly what happens in the very first act, when Canterbury, speaking for Henry's French claims, unfortunately echoes the biblical responses of the crowd to Pilate: "The sin upon my head" (1.2.97). (On Herod as "rant" see Hamlet's speech to the players. Shakespeare makes pointed use of the echoes from the account of Christ before Pilate in order to compromise Bolingbroke in *Richard II*.) If the same acts may be *interpreted* as exemplary for Christian counselors or Christian kings and worthy of the frenzied mob or of Herod, then they may rightly be considered to *be* neither in essence.

Coupling the idea of Herod's rant with the idea of Henry's Christian oratory breaks the necessary connection that would otherwise link an important signifier—the staged scene of Henry's oration—and its signified—the exemplary forensic ability and ethical restraint Henry embodies as model king. In this instance, then, the play handles an obviously iconic moment somewhat as Tarquin treats the symbolic events that offer to warn him away from Lucrece. And there is a more general sense in which the various iconoclastic elements of *Henry V* are related to the character of Tarquin. Tarquin's experience of remorse suggests that some truths can only be gathered along the strands of experience in time; thus, it is fitting that the iconoclastic elements of *Henry V* lead one to look before and after, to ask why and how, and for whom things are done. Instead of providing one with the tautological answers of icon, emblem, and allegory, the play prods one with questions, the very sorts of questions that had begun to haunt Tudor historical enquiry.

It is true that the general outline of historical biography during the English Renaissance usually kept close to the traditional forms of sacred hagiography. And it is also true that history plays like *Henry V* or *Henry IV* do seem to follow the schemata of saints' lives and related forms: in the one case reproducing those aspects of sacred literature that O. B. Hardison terms "ritual form," and in the other duplicating some of the features of the prodigal son stories. Furthermore, both Tudor history play and Tudor history do often resemble traditional hagiography in their readiness to treat matters of fact as secondary to didactic purpose and symbolic pageant. But, as Arthur B. Ferguson argues, Tudor history is marked by the emergence of an intense concern for details of cause and effect, particularities of historical context, and evidence of origins. It would be surprising indeed if this new impetus did not make itself felt in the works of a writer as well versed in historical study as was Shakespeare, since the general European current of which it is a part makes itself felt even in such unlikely places as Catholic hagiography and Calvinist aesthetics.

Rejecting the imaginary accretions of popular hagiography, which had substituted typical, idealized, personified abstractions for the historical individuality of the saints, the Bollandist scholars pursued the rigors of "historical method" even within the Church of Rome. While their forerunners had been content to represent iconic figures frozen into the stillness of "attitudes" dictated by attributes—their very beings imaginatively reconstituted from metaphors of conventional representation, as Joseph, forever virginal because he happens in paintings of the Holy Family to hold the lily symbolic of the Virgin Birth—the Bollandists sought instead the actions of the living individual, in a time, in a place. Such concerns created genuine tensions in the intellectual life of the sixteenth and seventeenth centuries—and in its art.

In fact, the relative merits of moment and movement, meaning and means, allegory and history constitute a major source of debate between Catholic and Calvinist positions on the visual arts. In the *Institutes* Calvin carefully discriminates between visual representations of "histories and events," which he allows as useful, and the portrayal of "images and forms of bodies without any depicting of past events," which he damns as debased products of human "craving." The mainline Catholic response to this distinction as expressed in the *Dictionnaire de théologie catholique* is interesting and worth quoting in full:

> Calvin accepte bien que l'on représente des scènes historiques qui relatent les actions vertueuses des saints, mais il ne veut point que l'on fasse des images de personnages isolés. D'abord, quel inconvénient y a-t-il? Ensuite, s'il est utile de nous remettre sous les yeux des actions vertueuses, il est pareillement utile de nous rappeler les saints qui les ont accomplies, indépendamment de telle ou telle action déterminée, et seulement avec la pensée générale de leur héroïsme sur la terre et de leur triomphe dans le ciel. Si ce souvenir est utile, pourquoi ne pas l'aider par l'image du saint, même représenté isolément? Du reste, assez souvent, les saints sont représentés dans une attitude

ou avec un attribut qui rappelle un souvenir plus précis. Le lis de saint Joseph nous parle de sa virginité et le gril de saint Laurent nous fait penser à son martyre.

Calvin accepts that one may represent historical scenes which report the virtuous acts of the saints, but he does not at all wish that one fashion images of isolated figures. First, what objection is there? Then, if it is useful to set virtuous acts before our eyes, it is similarly useful to remind ourselves of the saints who accomplished them, independently of this or that definite action, solely with the general idea of their heroism on this earth and their triumph in heaven. If such recollection is useful, why not aid it with the image of the saint, even if represented in isolation? Moreover, often enough, the saints are represented in an attitude or with an attribute that recalls a more precise memory. The lily of Saint Joseph tells us of his virginity and the grill of Saint Lawrence makes us think of his martyrdom.

Rejecting the Calvinist emphasis on "such and such a determinate action" in a certain and ascertainable historical context, the Catholic response acknowledges no important difference between such a highly particularized "historical" image and an image "generally" signifying some abstract quality through the presentation of a stylized "attitude" or "attribute."

Within *Henry V* these values are in conflict: the one confident that truth can be rendered in the iconic, the other insistent upon context and qualification. On the one hand, the play seems conceived as something like the bee's commonwealth, in that it seems to assume that many varied but related images may all find their place in a unified hierarchy of intended meanings:

> many things, having full reference
> To one consent, may work contrariously;
> As many arrows, loosed several ways,
> Come to one mark.
>
> (1.2.205–9)

And Henry's English warrior's Christian virtue is clearly their mark. On the other hand, there is the ironic enactment, best summed up in Fluellen's somewhat lower expression of the same idea:

> FLUELLEN: What call you the town's name where
> Alexander the Pig was born?
> GOWER: Alexander the Great.
> FLUELLEN: Why, I pray you, is not pig great? the pig, or
> the great, or the mighty, or the huge, or the mag-
> nanimous, are all one reckonings, save the phrase is
> a little variations.
>
> (4.7.14–19)

A little various the phrase, the element, the particular image may be from its prototypal concept! What a difference the difference between general fore-conceit and particular receipt makes. The breach between signifier and signified may be opened, as it is in this case, so far that the effect is not at all that of Lucrece's blood flowing into larger circles of significance and order, but rather that of an invasion whereby the citadel of significance is made vulnerable to violation. Even Henry's Aristotelian quality of true princely magnanimity is opened to reinterpretation in Fluellen's association of swinishness with power.

The fall of Lucrece's "sweet city" differs from the fall of Harfleur to the extent that the poetic dramatist has come to strengthen the force of Fluellen's second critical truism—"There is occasions and causes why and wherefore in all things" (5.1.3)—against his first—"there is figures in all things" (4.7.35). In *Julius Caesar* these modes of understanding grapple with each other with such near equality of strength that "oft they interchange each other's seat."

History and Ideology:
The Instance of *Henry V*

Jonathan Dollimore and Alan Sinfield

> *Behind the disorder of history Shakespeare assumed some kind of order or degree on earth having its counterpart in heaven. Further, . . . in so assuming he was using the thought-idiom of his age and could have avoided doing so only by not thinking at all.*
>
> E. M. W. TILLYARD, *Shakespeare's History Plays*

The objections are familiar enough: the "Elizabethan World Picture" simplifies the Elizabethans and, still more, Shakespeare. Yet if we look again at what Tillyard was opposing, his historicism seems less objectionable—assertions, for example, that Shakespeare does not "seem to call for explanations beyond those which a whole heart and a free mind abundantly supply"; that "he betrays no bias in affairs of church or state"; that "No period of English literature has less to do with politics than that during which English letters reached their zenith." All these quotations are taken by Lily B. Campbell from critics influential between the wars. She and Tillyard demonstrate unquestionably that there was an ideological position, something like "the Elizabethan World Picture," and that it is a significant presence in Shakespeare's plays. Unfortunately, inadequacies in their theorizing of ideology have set the agenda for most subsequent work. We shall argue initially that even that criticism which has sought to oppose the idea that Shakespeare believed in and expresses a political hierarchy whose rightness is guaranteed by its reflection of a divine

From *Alternative Shakespeares,* edited by John Drakakis. © 1985 by Jonathan Dollimore and Alan Sinfield. Methuen, 1985.

hierarchy, is trapped nevertheless in a problematic of order, one which stems from a long tradition of idealist philosophy.

Tillyard makes little of the fact that the writers he discusses were members of the class fraction of which the government of the country was constituted, or were sponsored by the government, or aspired to be. He seems not to notice that the *Homily against Disobedience and Wilful Rebellion* is designed to preserve an oppressive regime—he admires the "dramatic touch" at the start, "a splendid picture of original obedience and order in the Garden of Eden." His skills of critical analysis do not show him that the projection of an alleged human order onto an alleged divine order affords, in effect even if not intention, a mystifying confirmation of the *status quo*. On the contrary, he claims to show that Shakespeare was "the voice of his own age first and only through being that, the voice of humanity." In similar fashion, Campbell speaks of "the political philosophy of [Shakespeare's] age" as "universal truth":

> If, however, he is not merely a poet but a great poet, the particulars of his experience are linked in meaning to the universal of which they are a representative part . . . a passion for universal truth . . . takes his hatred and his love out of the realm of the petty and into the realm of the significant.

Of course, much critical energy has been spent on opposing Tillyard and Campbell; they were writing during the Second World War, and the idea that the great English writer propounded attitudes which tended to encourage acquiescence in government policy has come to seem less attractive subsequently. One point of view argues that Shakespeare saw through the Tudor Myth and, with it, all human aspirations and especially political aspirations. Shakespeare's plays are thus made to speak an absurdist or nihilist idea of the "human condition"—a precise reversal of the divinely guaranteed harmony proclaimed by Tillyard. A second point of view again argues the limitations of the Tudor Myth and the futility of politics, but asserts over and against these the possibility of individual integrity. This inhibits even more effectively specific consideration of how power works and how it may be challenged, since integrity may be exercised within—or, even better, over and against—any socio-political arrangements.

Anguish at the failure of the idea of order is represented most importantly by Jan Kott's *Shakespeare Our Contemporary* (1967). Kott sees that the Tudor Myth was always a political device, and he argues that the history plays disclose this. He sees also that the legitimacy or illegitimacy, the goodness or badness of the monarch, is not the real issue: "there are no bad kings, or good kings; kings are only kings. Or let us put it in modern terms: there is only the king's situation, and the system." Kott has here the basis for a materialist analysis of power and ideology, but then takes the argument towards the inevitable, all-encompassing inversion of cosmic order: "The implacable roller of history crushes everybody and everything. Man is determined by his situation, by the step of the grand staircase on which he happens to find himself." There seems to be no play in such a system—no scope for intervention, subversion, negotiation; analysis of specific historical process, with the enabling as well as the limiting possibilities within an ideological conjuncture, seems futile—the point being, precisely, that everything is pointless.

Kott does little more than invert the Elizabethan World Picture: the terms of the debate are not changed. As Derrida insists, a metaphysic of order is not radically undermined by invoking disorder; the two terms are necessary to each other, within the one problematic. Order is predicated on the undesirability of disorder, and vice versa. "Theatre of the Absurd," which Kott invokes in his chapter comparing *King Lear* to Beckett's *Endgame,* takes its whole structure from the absence of God, and therefore cannot but affirm the importance and desirability of God. Kott's approach has been influential, especially in the theatre, for it has chimed in with attention to modernist and existentialist writings which offer as profound studies of the human condition a critique of progressive ideals and an invocation of "spiritual" alienation.

The limitations of the Tudor Myth are pressed also by Wilbur Sanders in *The Dramatist and the Received Idea* (1968). Here the switch is not towards the futility of existence generally, but towards the priority of personal integrity. Like Kott, he sees the plays as showing political action to be essentially futile, and that there is an inevitability in historical process before which "even the best type of conservatism is ultimately powerless." But Sanders's next move is not into the absurd, but into a countervailing ideal order of individual integrity: the issue is how far any character "has been able to find a mature, responsible, fully human way of preserving his integrity in face of the threatening realities of political life." The selfish and inconsequential nature of this project, especially in so far as it is assigned to those who actually exercise power over others in their society, seems not to strike Sanders. Moreover, by refusing to discuss the political conditions within which integrity is to be exercised, he deprives his characters of knowledge which they would need to make meaningful choices; for instance, the decision York has to make between Richard II and Bolingbroke is structured by contradictions in the concept of monarchy and the position of regent, and York's integrity cannot be analysed sensibly without discussing those contradictions.

Sanders's position approaches the point where historical sequence, with all its injustice and suffering, may be regarded merely as a testing ground for the individual to mature upon. He seeks to fend off such anarchistic implications by declaring that "In Shakespeare's imagination the ideal social order, the mutuality of fulfilled human society, is inseparably bound up with the sacredness of the individual." Literary critics have tended to place much stress on the sacredness, and redemptive power of the individual, especially in discussions of the tragedies. G. K. Hunter summarizes what he calls the "modern" view of *King Lear:* it

> is seen as the greatest of tragedies because it not only strips
> and reduces and assaults human dignity, but because it also
> shows . . . the process of restoration by which humanity
> can recover from degradation. . . . [Lear's] retreat into the
> isolated darkness of his own mind is also a descent into the
> seed-bed of a new life; for the individual mind is seen here
> as a place from which a man's most important qualities and
> relationships draw the whole of their potential.
>
> (*Dramatic Identities and Cultural Tradition*)

Sanders's recourse to the individual is less confident than this; in fact, in places he remains poised uneasily between Kott and Tillyard, unable entirely to admit or repudiate the position of either. The characters he considers prove "seriously defective" and he is driven to acknowledge the possibility that Shakespeare is expressing "tragic cynicism." Thus, he veers towards Kott. To protect himself from this, and to posit some final ground for the integrity he demands, he swerves back towards something very like Tillyard's Christian humanism, wondering even "whether we can receive [the Elizabethans'] humane wisdom without their belief in absolutes." The entrapment of the Shakespearean characters is thus reproduced for the modern reader, who is required similarly to quest for an elusive wholeness within conditions whose determinants are to be neither comprehended nor challenged.

Perhaps the most fundamental error in all these accounts of the role of ideology is falsely to unify history and/or the individual human subject. In one, history is unified by a teleological principle conferring meaningful order (Tillyard), in another by the inverse of this—Kott's "implacable roller." And Sanders's emphasis on moral or subjective integrity implies a different though related notion of unity: an experience of subjective autonomy, of an essential self uncontaminated by the corruption of worldly process; "individual integrity" implies in the etymology of both words an ideal unity: the undivided, the integral.

Theories of the ultimate unity of both history and the human subject derive of course from a western philosophical tradition where, moreover, they have usually implied each other: the universal being seen as manifested through individual essences which, in turn, presuppose universals. Often unawares, idealist literary criticism has worked within or in the shadow of this tradition, as can be seen for example in its insistence that the universal truths of great literature are embodied in coherent and consistent "characters."

The alternative to this is not to become fixated on its negation—universal chaos and subjective fragmentation—but rather to understand history and the human subject in terms of social and political process. Crucial for such an understanding is a materialist account of ideology.

Ideology is composed of those beliefs, practices and institutions which work to legitimate the social order—especially by the process of representing sectional or class interests as universal ones. This process presupposes that there are others, subordinate classes, who far from sharing the interests of the dominant class are, in fact, being exploited by that class. This is one reason why the dominant tend not only to "speak for" subordinate classes but actively to repress them as well. This repression operates coercively but also ideologically (the two are in practice inseparable). So, for example, at the same time that the Elizabethan ruling fraction claimed to lead and speak for all, it persecuted those who did not fit in, even blaming them for the social instability which originated in its own policies. This is an instance of a process of displacement crucial then (and since) in the formation of dominant identities—class, cultural, racial and sexual.

Ideology is not just a set of ideas, it is material practice, woven into the fabric of everyday life. At the same time, the dominant ideology is realized specifically through the institutions of education, the family, the law, religion, journalism and culture. In the Elizabethan state, all these institutions worked to achieve ideological unity—not always successfully, for conflicts and contradictions remained visible at all levels, even within the dominant class fraction and its institutions. The theatre was monitored closely by the state—both companies and plays had to be licensed—and yet its institutional position was complex. On the one hand, it was sometimes summoned to perform at court and, as such, may seem a direct extension of royal power; on the other hand, it was the mode of cultural production in which market forces were strongest, and, as such, it was especially exposed to the influence of subordinate and emergent classes. We should not, therefore, expect any straightforward relationship between plays and ideology: on the contrary, it is even likely that the topics which engaged writers and audiences alike were those where ideology was under strain. We will take as an instance for study *Henry V,* and it will appear that even in this play, which is often assumed to be one where Shakespeare is closest to state propaganda, the construction of ideology is complex—even as it consolidates, it betrays inherent instability.

The principal strategy of ideology is to legitimate inequality and exploitation by representing the social order which perpetuates these things as immutable and unalterable—as decreed by God or simply natural. Since the Elizabethan period the ideological appeal to God has tended to give way to the equally powerful appeal to the natural. But in the earlier period both were crucial: the laws of degree and order inferred from nature were further construed as having been put there by God. One religious vision represented ultimate reality in terms of unity and stasis: human endeavour, governed by the laws of change and occupying the material domain, is ever thwarted in its aspiration, ever haunted by its loss of an absolute which can only be regained in transcendence, the move through death to eternal rest, to an ultimate unity inseparable from a full stasis, "when no more *Change* shall be" and "all shall rest eternally" (Spenser, *The Faerie Queene,* 7.2). This metaphysical vision has its political uses, especially when aiding the process of subjection by encouraging renunciation of the material world and a disregard of its social aspects such that oppression is experienced as a fate rather than an alterable condition. Protestantism tended to encourage engagement in the world rather than withdrawal from it; most of the *The Faerie Queene* is about the urgent questing of knights and ladies. The theological underpinning of this activist religion was the doctrine of callings: "God bestows his gifts upon us . . . that they might be employed in his service and to his glory, and that in this life" (E. William Perkins). This doctrine legitimated the expansive assertiveness of a social order which was bringing much of Britain under centralized control, colonizing parts of the New World and trading vigorously with most of the Old, and which was to experience revolutionary changes. At the same time, acquiescence in an unjust social order (like that encouraged by a fatalistic metaphysic of stasis) seemed to be effected, though less securely, by an insistence that "whatsoever any man enterpriseth or doth, either in word or deed, he must do it by virtue of his calling, and he must keep himself within the compass, limits or precincts thereof." This ideology was none the less metaphysical.

Such an activist ideology is obviously appropriate for the legitimation of warfare, and so we find it offered by the Archbishop of Canterbury in *Henry V*—as the Earl of Essex set off for Ireland in 1599 Lancelot Andrewes assured the Queen in a sermon that it was "a war sanctified." In the honeybees speech human endeavour is not denigrated but harnessed in an imaginary unity quite different from that afforded by stasis: "So may a thousand actions, once afoot, / End in one purpose" (1.2.211–12). Like so many political ideologies, this one shares something essential with the overtly religious metaphysic it appears to replace, namely a teleological explanation of its own image of legitimate power—that is, an explanation which is justified through the assertion that such power derives from an inherent natural and human order encoded by God. Thus, the "one purpose" derives from an order rooted in "a rule in nature" (1.2.188), itself a manifestation of "heavenly" creation, God's regulative structuring of the universe. What this inherent structure guarantees above all is, predictably, obedience:

> Therefore doth heaven divide
> The state of man in divers functions,
> Setting endeavour in continual motion;
> To which is fixed, as an aim or butt,
> Obedience.
> (1.2.183–87)

And what in turn underpins obedience is the idea of one's job or calling—in effect one's bee-like *function*—as following naturally from a God-given identity: soldiers,

> armed in their stings,
> Make boot upon the summer's velvet buds;
> Which pillage they with merry march bring home
> To the tent-royal of their emperor.
>
> (1.2.193–96)

The activist ideology thus displaces the emphasis on stasis yet remains thoroughly metaphysical none the less. More generally: in this period, perhaps more than any since, we can see a secular appropriation of theological categories to the extent that it may be argued that Reformation theology actually contributed to secularization; nevertheless, it was an appropriation which depended upon continuities, the most important of which, in ideological legitimation, is this appeal to teleology.

Not only the justification of the war but, more specifically, the heroic representation of Henry, works in such terms. His is a power rooted in nature—blood, lineage and breeding: "The blood and courage that renowned them / Runs in your veins" (1.2.118–19)—but also deriving ultimately from God's law as it is encoded in nature and, by extension, society: France belongs to him "by gift of heaven, / By law of nature and of nations" (2.4.79–80). Conversely, the French king's power is construed in terms of "borrow'd glories," "custom" and "mettle . . . bred out" (2.4.79, 83; 3.5.29). With this theory of legitimate versus illegitimate power the responsibility for aggression is displaced onto its victims. Thus does war find its rationale, injustice its justification.

There are two levels of disturbance in the state and the ideology which legitimates it: contradiction and conflict. Contradiction is the more fundamental, in the sense of being intrinsic to the social process as a whole—when for example the dominant order negates what it needs or, more generally, in perpetuating itself produces also its own negation. Thus, for example, in the seventeenth century the monarchy legitimates itself in terms of religious attitudes which themselves come to afford a justification for opposition to monarchy. We shall be observing contradiction mainly as it manifests itself in the attempts of ideology to contain it. Conflict occurs between opposed interests, either as a state of disequilibrium or as active struggle; it occurs along the structural fault lines produced by contradictions.

Ideology has always been challenged, not least by the exploited themselves, who have resisted its oppressive construction of them and its mystification of their disadvantaged social position. One concern of a materialist criticism is with the history of such resistance, with the attempt to recover the voices and cultures of the repressed and marginalized in history and writing. Moreover, ideology is destabilized not only from below, but by antagonisms within and among the dominant class or class fraction (high, as opposed to popular, literature will often manifest this kind of destabilization). Whereas idealist literary criticism has tended to emphasize the transcendence of conflict and contradiction, materialist criticism seeks to stay with them, wanting to understand them better.

Ideologies which represent society as a spurious unity must of necessity also efface conflict and contradiction. How successful they are in achieving this depends on a range of complex and interrelated factors, only a few of which we have space to identify here. One such will be the relative strength of emergent, subordinate and oppositional elements within society. The endless process of contest and negotiation between these elements and the dominant culture is often overlooked in the use of some structuralist perspectives within cultural analysis.

One other factor which militates against the success of ideological misrepresentation involves a contradiction fundamental to ideology itself (and this will prove specially relevant in *Henry V*): the more ideology (necessarily) engages with the conflict and contradiction which it is its *raison d'être* to occlude, the more it becomes susceptible to incorporating them within itself. It faces the contradictory situation whereby to silence dissent one must first give it a voice, to misrepresent it one must first present it.

These factors make for an inconsistency and indeterminacy in the representation of ideological harmony in writing: the divergencies have to be included if the insistence on unity is to have any purchase, yet at the same time their inclusion invites sceptical interrogation of the ideological appearance of unity, of the effacements of actual conflict. There may be no way of resolving whether one, or which one, of these tendencies (unity versus divergencies) overrides the other in a particular play, but in a sense it does not matter: there is here an indeterminacy which alerts us to the complex but always significant process of theatrical representation and, through that, of political and social process.

II

It is easy for us to assume, reading *Henry V,* that foreign war was a straightforward ground upon which to establish and celebrate national unity. In one sense this is so and it is the basic concern of the play. But in practice foreign war was the site of competing interests, material and ideological, and the assumption that the nation must unite against a common foe was shot through with conflict and contradiction. This was equally true for the hegemonic class fraction, though it was they who needed, urgently, to deny divisions and insist that everyone's purpose was the same. Queen Elizabeth feared foreign war because it was risky and expensive and threatened to disturb the fragile balance on which her power was founded. Members of the Privy Council favoured it—in some cases because it would strengthen their faction (puritans continually urged military support for continental protestants), in other cases because it would enhance their personal, military and, hence, political power. The Church resented the fact that it was expected to help finance foreign wars; but in 1588 Archbishop Whitgift encouraged his colleagues to contribute generously towards resistance to the Armada on the grounds—just as in *Henry V*—that it would head off criticism of the Church's wealth.

For the lower orders, war meant increased taxation, which caused both hardship and resentment, as Francis Bacon testified in Parliament in 1593. On the other hand, war profited some people, though in ways which hardly inspired national unity. Some officers took money in return for discharging mustered men and enlisting others instead—Essex complained in Star Chamber in 1596 that "the liege and free people of this realm are sold like cattle in a market." In 1589 Sir John Smith overheard two gentlemen joking that the recent military expedition against Spain "would be worth unto one of them above a thousand marks and to the other above £400 . . . by the death of so many of their tenants that died in the journey: that the new fines for other lives would be worth that or more." War, in these aspects, must have tended to discredit ideas of shared national purpose. Indeed, there are a number of reports of mutinous individuals asserting that poor people would do better under the King of Spain. This desperate inversion, whereby the demonized other of state propaganda was perceived as preferable, indicates the difficulty people have in envisaging alternatives to the existing power structure.

In fact, *Henry V* is only in one sense "about" national unity: its obsessive preoccupation is insurrection. The King is faced with actual or threatened insurrection from almost every quarter: the Church, "treacherous" fractions within the ruling class, slanderous subjects, and soldiers who undermine the war effort, either by exploiting it or by sceptically interrogating the King's motives. All these areas of possible resistance in the play had their counterparts in Elizabethan England and the play seems, in one aspect, committed to the aesthetic colonization of such elements in Elizabethan culture; systematically, antagonism is reworked as subordination or supportive alignment. It is not so much that these antagonisms are openly defeated but rather that they are represented as inherently submissive. Thus the Irish, Welsh and Scottish soldiers manifest not their countries' centrifugal relationship to England but an ideal subservience of margin to centre. Others in the play are seen to renounce resistance in favour of submission. Perhaps the most interesting instance of this is the full and public repentance of the traitors, Cambridge, Grey and Scroop. Personal confession becomes simultaneously a public acknowledgment of the rightness of that which was challenged. It is, of course, one of the most authoritative ideological legitimations available to the powerful: to be sincerely validated by former opponents—especially when their confessional self-abasement is in excess of what might be expected from the terms of their defeat.

Nevertheless, we should not assume inevitable success for such strategies of containment; otherwise how could there have been Catholic recusants, the Essex rebellion, enclosure riots? *Henry V* belongs to a period in which the ideological dimension of authority—that which helps effect the internalization rather than simply the coercion of obedience—is recognized as imperative and yet, by that self-same recognition, rendered vulnerable to demystification. For example, the very thought that the actual purpose of the war might be to distract from troubles at home would tend to undermine the purposed effect. The thought is voiced twice in *2 Henry IV*: it is part of the advice given to Hal by his father (4.5.212–15) and John of Lancaster envisages it in the final speech. It is suppressed in *Henry V*—yet it twice surfaces obliquely (2.1.90–92; 4.1.228–29).

At the height of his own programme of self-legitimation Henry "privately" declares his awareness of the ideological role of "ceremony" (4.1.242–45). In the same soliloquy Henry speaks his fear of deceptive obedience—masking actual antagonism. It is a problem of rule which the play represses and resolves and yet reintroduces here in a half-rationalized form, as the "hard condition! / Twin-born with greatness" is presented initially as the sheer burden of responsibility carried by the ruler, the loneliness of office, but then as a particular kind of fear. As the soliloquy develops its subtext comes to the fore, and it is the same subtext as that in the confrontation with Bates and Williams: the possibility, the danger of subjects who disobey. What really torments Henry is the inability to ensure obedience. His "greatness" is "subject to the breath / Of every fool," "instead of homage sweet" he experiences "poison'd flattery," and although he can coerce the beggar's knee he cannot fully control it (4.1.240–41, 256–57). Not surprisingly, he has bad dreams. The implication is that subjects are to be envied not because, as Henry suggests, they are more happy in fearing than (like him) being feared, but almost the reverse: because as subjects they cannot suffer the king's fear of being disobeyed and opposed. Henry indicates a paradox of power only to misrecognize its force by mystifying both kingship and subjection. His problem is structural, since the same ceremonies or role-playing which constitute kingship are the means by which real antagonisms can masquerade as obedience—"poison'd flattery." Hence, perhaps, the slippage at the end of the speech from relatively cool analysis of the situation of the labouring person (referred to initially as "private men," ll. 243–44) into an attack on him or her as "wretched slave . . . vacant mind . . . like a lackey" (ll. 274–79), and finally "slave" of "gross brain" (ll. 287–88).

The play circles obsessively around the inseparable issues of unity and division, inclusion and exclusion. Before Agincourt the idea of idle and implicitly disaffected people at home is raised (4.3. 16–18), but this is converted into a pretext for the King to insist upon his army as a "band of brothers" (4.3.60). Conversely, unity of purpose may be alleged and then undercut. The act 3 Chorus asks:

> who is he, whose chin is but enrich'd
> With one appearing hair, that will not follow
> These cull'd and choice-drawn cavaliers to France?
> (ll. 22–24)

But within fifty lines Nym, the Boy and Pistol are wishing they were in London.

However, the threat of disunity did not involve only the common people. That the king and the aristocracy have more interest in foreign wars and in the area of "England" produced by them than do the common people is easy enough for us to see now. But such a straightforward polarization does not yield an adequate account of the divergent discourses which inform *Henry V;* on the contrary, it accepts uncritically a principal proposition of Elizabethan state ideology, namely that the ruling class was coherent and unified in its purposes, a proposition necessary to the idea that the state could be relied upon to secure the peace of all its subjects. Evidence to the contrary was dangerous, helping to provoke the thought that most violence stemmed from the imposition of "order" rather than its lack.

In practice, however, power was not coherently distributed. The Elizabethan state was in transition from a feudal to a bourgeois structure, and this had entailed and was to entail considerable violent disruption. Whilst the aristocracy helped to sponsor the ideology of the monarch's supreme authority, it actually retained considerable power itself and the power of the crown probably decreased during Elizabeth's reign. Elizabeth could maintain her position only through political adroitness, patronage and force—and all these, the latter especially, could be exercised only by and through the aristocracy itself. Elizabeth could oppose the Earl of Leicester if supported by Burghley, or vice versa, but she could not for long oppose them both. After the death of Leicester in 1589 the power struggle was not so symmetrical. The rise of the youthful, charismatic and militarily impressive Earl of Essex introduced a new element: he rivalled the Queen herself, as Burghley and Leicester never did. The more service, especially military, Essex performed, the more he established a rival power base, and Elizabeth did not care for it. The Irish expedition was make or break for both; Essex would be away from court and vulnerable to schemes against him, but were he to return with spectacular success he would be unstoppable. In the event, he was not successful, and thus found himself pushed into a corner where he could see no alternative but direct revolt. The exuberance of *Henry V* leads most commentators to link it with the early stages of the Irish expedition when the successful return could be anticipated; the Chorus of act 5 (ll. 29–35) actually compares Henry's return to England with it and there are indeed parallels between Henry and Essex. Both left dangers at home when they went to war, besieged Rouen, sacked foreign towns, were taken to represent a revival of chivalry and national purpose; Essex was already associated with Bolingbroke. The crucial difference of course is that Essex is not the monarch. That is why Henry must be welcomed "much more, and much more cause." Henry is both general and ruler, and therefore the structural problem of the overmighty subject—the repeated theme of other plays—does not present itself.

The existence of such a profound structural flaw at the centre of state power affords a cardinal exemplification of why the representation of ideological containment so often proves complex and ambiguous. The pyramid of the Tudor Myth was under strain at its very apex, for the legitimate ruler was not the most powerful person—the same issue promotes the action of *Henry VI, Macbeth* and many other plays. *Henry V* was a powerful Elizabethan fantasy simply because it represented a single source of power in the state. Nothing is allowed to compete with the authority of the King. The noblemen are so lacking in distinctive qualities that they are commonly reorganized or cut in production. And the point where the issue might have presented itself—the plot of Cambridge, Scroop and Grey—is hardly allowed its actual historical significance. Holinshed makes it plain that Cambridge's purpose in conspiring against Henry was to exalt to the crown Edmund Mortimer and after that himself and his family; that he did not confess this because he did not want to incriminate Mortimer and cut off this possibility; that Cambridge's son was to claim the crown in the time of Henry VI and that this Yorkist claim was eventually successful. Cambridge makes only an oblique reference to this structural fault in the state (2.2.155–57). The main impression we receive is that the conspirators were motivated by greed and incomprehensible evil—according to Henry, like "Another fall of man" (l. 142). Such arbitrary and general "human" failings obscure the kind of instability in the ruling fraction to which the concurrent career of Essex bore witness.

That the idea of a single source of power in the state was, if not a fantasy, a rare and precarious achievement is admitted in the epilogue. The infant Henry VI succeeded, "Whose state so many had the managing, / That they lost France and made his England bleed" (ll. 11–12). Many managers disperse power and unity falls apart.

The aristocracy is the most briskly handled of the various agents of disruption. Whether this is because it was the least or the most problematic is a fascinating question, but one upon which we can only speculate. *Henry V* far more readily admits of problems in the role of the Church, though the main effect of this is again to concentrate power, now spiritual as well as secular, upon the King. The Archbishop's readiness to use the claim to France to protect the Church's interests tends to discredit him and the Church, but this allows the King to appropriate their spiritual authority. Thus power which, in actuality, was distributed unevenly across an unstable fraction of the hegemonic class is drawn into the person of the monarch; he becomes its sole source of expression, the site and guarantee of ideological unity. This is a crucial effect of a process already identified, namely a complex, secular appropriation of the religious metaphysic in the legitimation of war:

> his wildness, mortified in him,
> Seem'd to die too; yea, at that very moment,
> Consideration like an angel came,
> And whipp'ed th'offending Adam out of him.
> (1.1.26–29)

The language is that of the Prayer Book service of Baptism: Henry takes over from the Church sacramental imagery which seems to transcend all worldly authority. Thus he is protected at once from any imputation of irreligion which might seem to arise from a preparedness to seize Church property, and he becomes the representative of the personal piety which adhered only doubtfully to the bishops. In him contradictions are resolved or transcended. This presumably is why the clerics are not needed after act 1. From the beginning and increasingly, Henry's appeals to God, culminating in the insistence that "God fought for us" (4.8.122), enact the priestly role as Andrewes in his sermon on the Essex expedition identified it. He observed that in successful Old Testament wars "a captain and a Prophet sorted together": the two roles are drawn into the single figure of Henry V.

On the eve of Agincourt Henry gives spiritual counsel to his soldiers:

> Every subject's duty is the king's; but every subject's soul
> is his own. Therefore should every soldier in the wars do
> as every sick man in his bed, wash every mote out of his
> conscience; and dying so, death is to him advantage; or not

> dying, the time was blessedly lost wherein such prepara-
> tion was gained
>
> (4.1.182–89)

It is the high point of Henry's priestly function, the point at which
the legitimation which religion could afford to the state is most fully
incorporated into a single ideological effect. Yet Henry is defensive
and troubled by the exchange and Williams is not satisfied. What has
happened, surely, is that the concentration of ideological power upon
Henry seems to amount also to concentration of responsibility:

> Upon the king! let us our lives, our souls,
> Our debts, our careful wives,
> Our children, and our sins lay on the king!
>
> (4.1.236–38)

In the play the drive for ideological coherence has systematically
displaced the roles of Church and aristocracy and nothing seems to
stand between the king and the souls of his subjects who are to die in
battle.

The issue is handled in two main ways by Henry. First, he
reduces it to the question of soldiers who have committed serious
crimes, for which Henry can then refuse responsibility; initial questions about widows and orphans (4.1.141–43) slip out of sight. Second, the distinction between him and his subjects is effaced by his
insistence that "the king is but a man" (4.1.101–2) and that he himself gains nothing, indeed loses from the power structure:

> O ceremony, show me but thy worth!
> What is thy soul of adoration?
> Art thou aught else but place, degree, and form.
> Creating awe and fear in other men?
> Wherein thou art less happy, being fear'd,
> Than they in fearing.
>
> (4.1.250–55)

Here the king himself is collapsed, syntactically, into the mere shows
of ceremony: "thou" in the third line quoted refers to "ceremony,"
in the fifth to Henry, and he slips from one to the other without the
customary formal signals. The effect, if we credit it, is to leave
"place, degree, and form," "awe and fear" standing without the
apparent support of human agency: Henry engrosses in himself the

ideological coherence of the state and then, asked to take responsibility for the likely defeat of Agincourt, claims to be an effect of the structure which he seemed to guarantee.

The act 2 Chorus wants to proclaim unity: "honour's thought / Reigns solely in the breast of every man"—but is rapidly obliged to admit treachery: "O England! . . . Were all thy children kind and natural!" (ll. 3–4, 16, 19). The following scene is not however about Cambridge, Scroop and Grey, but Nym, Bardolph and Pistol. This disputatious faction proves much more difficult to incorporate than the rebel nobility. Increasingly, since *2 Henry IV*, sympathy for these characters has been withdrawn; from this point on there seems to be nothing positive about them. It is here that Fluellen enters, offering an alternative to Falstaff among the lesser gentry and an issue—the control of England over the British Isles—easier to cope with. Fluellen may be funny, old-fashioned and pedantic, but he is totally committed to the King and his purposes, as the King recognizes (4.1.83–84). The low characters are condemned not only to death but to exclusion from national unity; it is as if they have had their chance and squandered it. Gower describes Pistol as "a gull, a fool, a rogue, that now and then goes to the wars to grace himself at his return into London under the form of a soldier" (3.6.68–70) and Bardolph endorses the identification:

> Well, bawd I'll turn,
> And something lean to cut-purse of quick hand.
> To England will I steal, and there I'll steal:
> And patches will I get unto these cudgell'd scars,
> And swear I got them in the Gallia wars.
> (5.1.89–93)

This group, disbanded soldiers, was a persistent danger and worry in Elizabethan society; William Hunt suggests that "embittered veterans and deserters brought back from the Low Countries the incendiary myth of an army of avengers" (*The Puritan Moment*). Two proclamations were issued in 1589 against "the great outrages that have been, and are daily committed by soldiers, mariners and others that pretend to have served as soldiers, upon her Highness' good and loving subjects"; martial law was instigated to hang offenders. The Elizabethan state was prepared to exclude from its tender care such persons, perhaps exemplifying the principle whereby dominant groups identify themselves by excluding or expelling others; not only are the virtues necessary for membership identified by contrast with the vices of the excluded. That Pistol has this degree of significance is suggested by the play's reluctance to let him go. He is made to discredit himself once more at Agincourt (4.4) and in his final confrontation with Fluellen he is clumsily humiliated (5.1).

Despite the thorough dismissal of Bardolph, Nym and Pistol, *Henry V* does not leave the issue of lower-class disaffection. If those characters must be abandoned because unworthy or incapable of being incorporated into the unified nation, yet others must be introduced who will prove more tractable.

The issue of the English domination of Wales, Scotland and Ireland appears in the play to be more containable, though over the centuries it may have caused more suffering and injustice than the subjection of the lower classes. The scene of the four captains (3.3) seems to effect an effortless incorporation, one in which, as Philip Edwards has pointed out, the Irish Macmorris is even made to protest that he does not belong to a distinct nation (*Threshold of a Nation*). The English captain, of course, is more sensible than the others. Most attention is given to Fluellen—Wales must have seemed the most tractable issue, for it had been annexed in 1536 and the English church and legal system had been imposed; Henry V and the Tudors could indeed claim to be Welsh. The jokes about the way Fluellen pronounces the English language are, apparently, for the Elizabethan audience and many since, an adequate way of handling the repression of the Welsh language and culture; the annexation of 1536 permitted only English speakers to hold administrative office in Wales.

Ireland was the great problem—the one Essex was supposed to resolve. The population was overwhelmingly Catholic and liable to support a continental invader, and resistance to English rule proved irrepressible, despite or more probably because of the many atrocities committed against the people—such as the slaughter of all the six hundred inhabitants of Rathlin Island by John Norris and Francis Drake in 1575. The assumption that the Irish were a barbarous and inferior people was so ingrained in Elizabethan England that it seemed only a natural duty to subdue them and destroy their culture. Indeed, at one level their ideological containment was continuous with the handling of the disaffected lower-class outgroup (a proclamation of 1594 dealt together with vagabonds who begged "upon pretense of service in the wars without relief" and "men of Ireland that have these late years unnaturally served as rebels against her majesty's forces beyond the seas"). But much more was at stake in the persistent Irish challenge to the power of the Elizabethan state, and it should be related to the most strenuous challenge to the English unity in *Henry V*: like Philip Edwards, we see the attempt to conquer France and the union in peace at the end of the play as a re-presentation of the attempt to conquer Ireland and the hoped-for unity of Britain. The play offers a displaced, imaginary resolution of one of the state's most intractable problems.

Indeed, the play is fascinating precisely to the extent that it is implicated in and can be read to disclose both the struggles of its own historical moment and their ideological representation. To see the play in such terms is not at all to conclude that it is merely a deluded and mystifying ideological fantasy. We observed that the King finally has difficulty, on the eve of Agincourt, in sustaining the responsibility which seems to belong with the ideological power which he has engrossed to himself: thus the fantasy of establishing ideological unity in the sole figure of the monarch arrives in an impasse which it can handle only with difficulty. As we have argued, strategies of containment presuppose centrifugal tendencies, and how far any particular instance carries conviction cannot be resolved by literary criticism. If we attend to the play's different levels of signification rather than its implied containments, it becomes apparent that the question of conviction is finally a question about the diverse conditions of reception. How far the King's argument is to be credited is a standard question for conventional criticism, but a materialist analysis takes several steps back and reads real historical conflict in and through his ambiguities. Relative to such conflict, the question of Henry's integrity becomes less interesting.

If *Henry V* represents the fantasy of a successful Irish campaign it also offers, from the very perspective of that project, a disquietingly excessive evocation of suffering and violence:

> If not, why, in a moment look to see
> The blind and bloody soldier with foul hand
> Defile the locks of your shrill-shrieking daughters;
> Your fathers taken by the silver beards,
> And their most reverend heads dash'd to the walls;
> Your naked infants spitted upon pikes,
> Whiles the mad mothers with their howls confus'd

> Do break the clouds, as did the wives of Jewry
> At Herod's bloody-hunting slaughtermen.
>
> (3.3.33–41)

This reversal of Henry's special claim to Christian imagery—now he is Herod against the Innocents—is not actualized in the play (contrary to the sources, in which Harfleur is sacked), but its rhetoric is powerful and at Agincourt the prisoners are killed (4.6.37). Here and elsewhere, the play dwells upon imagery of slaughter to a degree which disrupts the harmonious unity towards which ideology strives. So it was with Ireland: even those who, like the poet Edmund Spenser, defended torture and murder expressed compunction at the effects of English policy:

> they were brought to such wretchedness, as that any stony heart would have rued the same. Out of every corner of the woods and glens they came creeping forth upon their hands, for their legs would not bear them. . . . They did eat of the dead carions.
>
> (A View of the Present State of Ireland)

The human cost of imperial ambition protruded through even its ideological justifications, and the government felt obliged to proclaim that its intention was not "an utter extirpation and rooting out of that nation." The claim of the state to be the necessary agent of peace and justice was manifestly contradicted. Ireland was, and remains, its bad conscience.

Henry V can be read to reveal not only the strategies of power but also the anxieties informing both them and their ideological representation. In the Elizabethan theatre to foreground and even to promote such representations was not to foreclose on their interrogation. We might conclude from this that Shakespeare was indeed wonderfully impartial on the question of politics (as the quotations in our opening paragraph claim); alternatively, we might conclude that the ideology which saturates his texts, and their location in history, are the most interesting things about them.

Fathers, Sons, and Brothers in *Henry V*

Peter Erickson

The problem many readers face in relation to *Henry V* is "what to make of a diminished thing." One group praises it while another faults it for being a one-dimensional epic pageant; but both groups share the assumption that the complexity of the *Henry IV* plays is drastically reduced or altogether eliminated in *Henry V*. I reject this assumption and argue that in this final play of the second tetralogy, the locus of complexity has shifted. It no longer resides in the inter-relationships among the four major characters—Henry IV, Falstaff, Hotspur, and Hal—but is now relocated within the dominant central consciousness of the single remaining character—Henry V—who has in effect absorbed the other three. This absorption ensures the continuing resonance of the missing figures. Henry IV functions as a source of stress and tension in the new king's language in *Henry V*. Henry V's identity is defined in relation to his father and his father's projects—a connection that makes the son vulnerable as well as powerful. Henry V lacks a separate, independent self whose voice can be clearly identified and trusted as his own. The self at cross-purposes is registered in the crosscurrents in Henry V's language, which is far more interesting and haunting than has been acknowledged.

One of the chief obstacles to a fresh, full reading of *Henry V* is the formulation of a sharp opposition between Henry V's public role and his private voice, concluding that the latter has vanished. The notion that Henry V is so totally consumed by his role as king that

From *Patriarchal Structures in Shakespeare's Drama.* © 1985 by the Regents of the University of California. University of California Press, 1985.

the man is squeezed out is a simplified and inaccurate way to speak about the intricacies of his character; it does not ring true to the intensity of his language and imagery or to our intimacy with him. The idiosyncratic personal voice may be constrained and turbid, but it is still unmistakably there. Henry V's speeches cannot be read (or heard in the theater) exclusively as public oration because this approach ignores or underestimates the involuted quality of his rhetoric. His speeches have an effect of soliloquy. They are technically addressed to others, but only the cinema—distorting text and theatrical conditions—can create a completely convincing illusion of a public setting. Because of their sheer length, the speeches turn inward and gain a life of their own partly detached from the particular external circumstance. The emotionally involved linguistic structures in which the king embroils himself convey a feeling of isolation that makes them reverberate with self-doubt and self-questioning. The king's remark to Erpingham—"I and my bosom must debate a while" (4.1.31)—applies more generally to all his long speeches.

The momentary outburst in the soliloquy on ceremony in act 4, scene 1, is not an exception because the inner pressures on Henry V's public rhetoric have been building up gradually and continuously to that breaking point. For example, in act 2, scene 2, the king sets a trap to expose the three traitors, but the rhetorical overkill of his excessively lengthy peroration (ll. 79–144) communicates self-exposure. His calculated description of the traitors as Actaeons begins to sound reflexive: "For your own reasons turn into your bosoms, / As dogs upon their masters, worrying you" (ll. 82–83). The king's language typically suggests this "worrying" effect, as though he is overdoing it, is trying too hard, and is on the verge of losing control. We are often left with the impression that Henry V is not entirely convinced of the role his own rhetoric strains to enact. The apparent inauthenticity in his eloquence communicates not the emptiness of a hollow man but rather the fullness of Henry V's distress and anguish. We are made to feel the presence (not simply the absence) of the "naked frailties" that underlie his "manly readiness."

I

Before considering the vestige of Henry IV in *Henry V*, let us first trace the interdependence of father and son through the second tetralogy. In *Richard II*, Bolingbroke's first act as Henry IV is anxiously to call for his son. Lacking Richard II's multiplicity of inner selves, Henry IV uses Hal as an extension of himself on which to project incipient guilt about the deposition: "Can no man tell me of my unthrifty son? / 'Tis full three months since I did see him last. / If any plague hang over us, 'tis he" (5.3.1–3). In the first face-to-face meeting between Henry IV and Hal in *1 Henry IV,* father and son act as each other's conscience. The king begins by accusing Hal of being "the hot vengeance, and the rod of heaven, / To punish my mistread-ings" (3.2.10–11) and then criticizes him for his failure to repeat the king's own success story. From the perspective of the audience, the irony lies in how much Hal is already his father's son. We have overheard Hal conceive a rise to power predicated on tactical calcu-lations similar to his father's. Both men use festive ritual as a meta-phor for creating a strategic impression. "But when they [holidays] seldom come, they wish'd for come, / And nothing pleaseth but rare accidents" (1.2.206–7) has its counterpart in "and so my state, / Seldom but sumptuous, show'd like a feast / And wan by rareness such solemnity" (3.2.57–59).

In taking on the role of his father in the "play extempore," Hal had labeled Falstaff "that father ruffian" (2.4.454) and clearly fore-shadowed the eventual banishment: "I do, I will" (l. 481). Given this clarity, how can we account for the difficulties in the relationship between Henry IV and Hal? Neither father nor son can securely know exactly who the other is because of his theatrical sense of himself. Each sees himself through the eyes of the spectators and thinks in terms of staging maximum visual impact. Just as Hal en-visions himself as a sun "breaking through the foul and ugly mists" (1.2.202), so his father describes himself as a comet and as "sunlike majesty / When it shines seldom in admiring eyes" (3.2.47, 79–80). Henry IV also uses clothing imagery to explain his self-presentation: "And dress'd myself in such humility," "Thus did I keep my person fresh and new, / My presence, like a robe pontifical, / Ne'er seen but wond'red at" (ll. 51, 55–57). This manipulation of public ap-pearance, which proves politically successful for both father and son, constitutes a barrier in their relationship with each other. Yet at the same time the intense desire to remove all artifice is manifested when Hal reiterates his allegiance to his father:

> I will redeem all this on Percy's head
> And in the closing of some glorious day

> Be bold to tell you that I am your son,
> When I will wear a garment all of blood,
> And stain my favors in a bloody mask,
> Which wash'd away shall scour my shame with it.
>
> (ll. 132–37)

The possibility that "garment" and "mask" can be "wash'd away" suggests the longing to restore purity both to divine kingship and to the personal relationship between father and son.

The parallel meeting in *2 Henry IV* has the same agenda of dealing with guilt and follows the same cyclical pattern of paternal recrimination, filial submission, and final atonement. In both *1 Henry IV* and *2 Henry IV*, Henry IV opens with a sarcastic, self-pitying castigation of his son, which is followed by the son's promise to live up to his father's highest expectations, followed by swift reconciliation, followed by the dispatch of business. In view of Warwick's confidence that "The Prince will in the perfectness of time / Cast off his followers" (*2H4*, 4.4.74–75), the lengthy negotiation between father and son may seem unnecessary. Yet while Warwick's attitude serves to underscore Henry IV's lack of perception, Warwick's perspective is in turn limiting. His clear-cut sense of Hal's obvious dedication is of little help in understanding Shakespeare's remarkably inclusive idea of politics. The myth that Henry IV and Henry V are consummate politicians who have no time or taste for feelings is belied by the way private emotions are insisted upon as part of the intimate transmission of political power. Warwick's reasonable account is inadequate because Henry IV must talk to Hal in person; Hal is the only person who can complete the transaction.

It is extraordinary how, even at the moment when loyalty is being declared, the image of parricide stands forth so vividly:

> Thus, my most royal liege,
> Accusing it, I put it on my head,
> To try with it, as with an enemy
> That had before my face murdered my father,
> The quarrel of a true inheritor.
>
> (4.5.164–68)

The crown becomes a third person through whose medium father and son can exchange and deflect violent anger while at the same time they are reconciled with each other. Henry IV summarizes his delight at the argument's outcome: "God put it in thy mind to take it hence, / That thou mightst win the more thy father's love, / Pleading so wisely in excuse of it!" (ll. 178–80). The particular phrasing of "win," "pleading," and "excuse" suggests a Lear-like demand that Hal's protests of devotion successfully gratify and placate.

It soon becomes clear that Henry IV's anger with Hal was a preliminary manifestation of his own guilt about the deposing of Richard II. Having elicited Hal's support, Henry IV is now able to relieve this sense of guilt directly by confiding it. The paradox of atonement is that Hal has gained his father's blessing instead of his initial curse, but the blessing itself is burdened, through the father's confession, with the potential curse of a tainted crown. It is within this crux that we can experience the peculiar nature of Hal's identification with his father. Hal as Henry V will not be an exact replica of Henry IV; rather, he becomes the father in the special sense of trying to be better than the father. This striving for improvement entails acceptance of the father since purification is Henry IV's express wish for his son. The permission is also an injunction. Henry V must surpass his father because that is the prearranged means of atoning with and for him.

In the standard psychoanalytic formulation developed by Ernst Kris in "Prince Hal's Conflict" (*Psychoanalytic Explorations in Art,* 1948), Kris describes "the formulation of the superego":

> The Prince, in his thoughts, compares the King, his father, with an ideal of royal dignity far superior to the father himself. This ideal, derived from paternal figures but exalted and heightened, is his protection in the struggle against his parricidal impulses and against submission to the King.

However, Hal–Henry V does not succeed in avoiding "submission to the King." The "ideal of royal dignity far superior to the father himself" is Henry IV's directive to his son at the moment of atonement. Hal does not simply use "his ideal of moral integrity as a reproachful contrast against his father" since their reunion is based on sharing this ideal. The reconciliation made possible by Hal's expression of duty and love is also a burden: "Aeneas *patrem umeris portans,* carrying one's father on one's back; a super-ego, which is also a historical destiny" (Norman O. Brown). Along with the ideals of redemption and integrity, a sense of sin is inherited through Henry IV's acknowledgment of the impurities in his succession to the kingship. The pragmatic advice about how "to busy giddy minds / With foreign quarrels" (*2H4*, 4.5.213–14) tacitly concedes doubt about whether his "death / Changes the mood" (ll. 198–99). Thus, the atonement consists of both the insistence on purging evil and the original evil. This dual genesis of purification and guilt—in relation to the father—may be understood as the fashioning of Henry V's reformation conscience.

Henry V's first speech after his father's death moves back and forth between acknowledging the appropriateness of mourning and arguing against the need for it. Surprisingly, the primary message is Henry V's gaiety. The traditional paradox—Le roi est mort; vive le roi!—has a special twist here because of the father-son identification that Henry V's exhilaration conveys in the punning on Harry: "Yet weep that Harry's dead, and so will I, / But Harry lives, that shall convert those tears / By number into hours of happiness" (5.2.59–61). As "the person of your father" and "the image of his power" (ll. 73–74), the lord chief justice symbolizes the survival of the dead king and serves as the means by which Hal's private submission to his father can be translated into an institutional norm. The renewal of Henry IV in Henry V's kingship is implied by casting the lord chief justice in a paternal posture, which is then internalized: "You shall be as a father to my youth, / My voice shall sound as you do prompt mine ear" (ll. 118–19). The extent of Henry V's incorporation of his father is most forcefully stated by direct invocation: "My father is gone wild into his grave, / For in his tomb lie my affections, / And with his spirits sadly I survive" (ll. 123–25). The earlier stress on "happiness" (l. 61) is now disrupted by a more somber implication. Father and son are so intertwined that their sacrifice is mutual; we cannot say that the father, as scapegoat, carries off the son's "affections" (l. 124) without also noting that the son "sadly" carries on his father's "spirits" (l. 125).

Emphasis on Hal's choice of loyalty to his father over subversive alliance with Falstaff is not, however, the most fruitful way to see the *Henriad*. A sense of guilt informs both the atonement with Henry IV and the banishment of Falstaff, and the simultaneous occurrence of these two events at the close of *2 Henry IV* should be treated as a single comprehensive gesture. Total embrace and total rejection are united as the two extreme, polar actions available to Hal-Henry V's guilt-ridden conscience. This sense of guilt underlies the epic surface of *Henry V*. We are faced in the final play of the second tetralogy with the paradox that although neither Falstaff nor Henry IV is actually present, both their presences are felt nonetheless. Both are scapegoats who refuse to stay away. Allusions to Falstaff and to Henry IV are trouble spots that make us feel uncomfortable about the official military victory, though they certainly do not prevent it. The net effect is to reopen the issues that Henry V had appeared to have conclusively resolved at the end of *2 Henry IV*.

Falstaff's absence in *Henry V* is made obtrusive by Quickly's narration of his death in act 2, scene 3. His banishment is amusingly but awkwardly recalled in the midst of the battle of Agincourt by Fluellen's methodical Plutarchan parallel. When Fluellen says of "the fat knight with the great belly doublet"—"I have forgot his name" (4.7.48–50), we can readily supply the answer. Like Henry IV, Falstaff retains the ghostlike capacity to resurrect himself at a critical moment. Despite his insistence on the differences between Alexander the Pig and Harry of Monmouth, Fluellen's mispronunciation and his thesauruslike dwelling on Alexander's "rages, and his furies, and his wraths, and his cholers, and his moods, and his displeasures, and his indignations" (ll. 34–36) produce comic embarrassment rather than comic relief. Finally, we are reminded of Falstaff through the lesser remaining versions of him in the progeny consisting of Pistol, Bardolph, and Nym, all of whom receive banishmentlike treatment.

Henry IV is evoked at the outset of *Henry V* by Canterbury's rhapsodic marveling over the way the new king's purity commenced with his father's death:

> The breath no sooner left his father's body,
> But that his wildness, mortified in him,
> Seem'd to die too; yea, at that very moment,
> Consideration like an angel came
> And whipt th' offending Adam out of him,
> Leaving his body as a paradise
> T' envelop and contain celestial spirits.
> Never was such a sudden scholar made;
> Never came reformation in a flood
> With such a heady currance, scouring faults;
> Nor never Hydra-headed willfulness
> So soon did lose his seat (and all at once)
> As in this king.
>
> (1.1.25–37)

Henry V's own account in *2 Henry IV* (5.2.123–29) is explicitly carried into the new play and embellished by Canterbury's review. The crescendo of triple "nevers" that round off his speech draws our attention to the embellishment. This hyperbolic image of Henry V's perfect soul is sometimes taken as an achieved reality, but the archbishop's prominently placed speech names the play's agenda only in the sense that it announces a theme to be probed dramatically. The king as an actual character, though sensitive to matters of conscience, never assumes the paradisal poise with the ease Canterbury suggests here. Ultimately, Henry V is deprived of this pleasant angelic image when, before Agincourt, he is forced to face the negative side of his relationship with his father. But even Canterbury cannot believe in the miracle wrought by his own rhetoric: "for miracles are ceas'd; / And therefore we must needs admit the means / How things are perfected" (1.1.67–69). If Hal's "veil of wildness" (l. 64) is a strategy belonging to "the art and practic part of life" (l. 51), so may be his spectacular "reformation" (l. 33). Somewhere between the masks of wildness and of angelic consideration may lie the truth of Henry V's identity, which cannot be uttered in the "sweet and honeyed sentences" "men's ears" (ll. 50, 49) are so ready to consume.

The drama of the new king's identity is presented as a tension between two versions of paternal inheritance. The first is a heroic call that sidesteps the guilt associated with Henry IV and recovers an earlier father, Edward III. Canterbury absolves the king's conscience by shifting from a religious to a military vision:

> Stand for your own, unwind your bloody flag,
> Look back into your mighty ancestors;
> Go, my dread lord, to your great-grandsire's tomb,
> From whom you claim; invoke his warlike spirit,
> And your great-uncle's, Edward the Black Prince,
> Who on the French ground play'd a tragedy,
> Making defeat on the full power of France,
> Whiles his most mighty father on a hill
> Stood smiling to behold his lion's whelp
> Forage in blood of French nobility.
>
> (1.2.101–10)

If Henry V can perform the role of son by duplicating the Black Prince's feat, he can win the unqualified approval of the watchful, powerful father. As the play metaphor attests, this prospect involves the calculated construction of an identity, one offering physical danger but relative psychological safety. The son will "play a tragedy" at which the father will "smile"; this model of father–son relations produces a style of conscience so immune (or so impervious) that it mixes genres with impunity, freely converting aggression into pleasure.

The appeal of Edward III and of the Black Prince is kept before us by subsequent references. The French king echoes Canterbury's account (2.4.50–64); Henry V's claim points to "this most memorable line" (2.4.88), a "pedigree" proving him "evenly deriv'd / From his most fam'd of famous ancestors, / Edward the Third" (ll. 90–93); finally, Fluellen dutifully echoes the chronicle sources (4.7.92–95). Yet Henry V is unable simply to fulfill the destiny promised to him as a "heroical seed" (2.4.59) because he cannot completely disregard the more problematic alternative: the image, closer to home, of his own father. Initially, the play skirts this difficulty, glancing at "the scambling and unquiet time" during "the last king's reign" (1.1.4, 2). Henry V preserves the ideal of a purified and unified England by ordering the death of the conspirator who falsely remarked: "those that were your father's enemies / Have steep'd their galls in honey, and do serve you / With hearts create of duty and of zeal" (2.2.29–31). But prior to the climactic battle at Agincourt, the king trips on his own logic and stumbles into a painful confrontation with the lingering issue of his father's guilty conscience.

Pressed to defend his "cause" (4.1.127) to the common soldiers while in the "shape" of "a common man" (4.8.53, 50), Henry V resorts to the metaphor of father and son: "So, if a son that is by his father sent about merchandise do sinfully miscarry upon the sea, the imputation of his wickedness, by your rule, should be impos'd upon his father that sent him. . . . But this is not so" (4.1.147–55). His argument, in keeping the sins of the son from being visited on the father, strictly separates their destinies. In the soliloquy soon to follow, when he protects himself from his father's sins, Henry V tries to insist on the same absolute separation. He attempts to admit his father's "fault" while simultaneously suspending it so that he cannot be contaminated: "Not to-day, O Lord, / O, not to-day, think not upon the fault / My father made in compassing the crown!" (ll. 292–94). The weakness of this effort is indicated by the plea to "think not upon"—purity can now be achieved only by consciously ignoring the impurities of which Henry V is in fact acutely aware.

In soliloquy, Henry V pursues his original purpose—"I and my bosom must debate a while" (4.1.31)—with a seriousness he had not intended. However effectively he comports himself when placed on the spot by the common soldiers, the king is riled by their challenge. In debate with his men, he deflects attention away from his own responsibility by insisting on theirs: "Every subject's duty is the King's, but every subject's soul is his own. Therefore should every soldier in the wars do as every sick man in his bed, wash every mote out of his conscience" (ll. 176–80). Thrown back on himself in soliloquy, Henry V sharply reverses himself, taking on the sin he has been at pains to keep at bay:

> Upon the King! let us our lives, our souls,
> Our debts, our careful wives,
> Our children, and our sins lay on the King!
> We must bear all.
>
> (230–33)

The king portrays himself as a scapegoat only sarcastically, out of frustration. The sins are still his subjects', not his. Yet Henry V's attack on the symbols of the regal power he has inherited suggests a more personal grappling with his own conscience.

The second part of his soliloquy is more specific in naming the source of sin:

> I Richard's body have interred new,
> And on it have bestowed more contrite tears,
> Than from it issued forced drops of blood.
> Five hundred poor I have in yearly pay,
> Who twice a day their wither'd hands hold up
> Toward heaven, to pardon blood; and I have built
> Two chauntries, where the sad and solemn priests
> Sing still for Richard's soul. More will I do;
> Though all that I can do is nothing worth,
> Since that my penitence comes after all,
> Imploring pardon.
>
> (4.1.295–305)

Henry V's generalized railing against the helplessness of "idol Ceremony" (l. 240) is now given concrete meaning by this enumeration of ritual activities for Richard II. The mechanical and quantitative nature of the ceremony, Henry V's flat, weary tone in reviewing it, and his direct confession of failure—"all that I can do is nothing worth"—indicate the hoplessness of his attempt at expiation. Nevertheless, he tries to contain the eruption of guilt by labeling it his father's problem: it is "the fault / My father made" rather than his own fault. Henry V's genuinely "contrite tears" (l. 296) are futile "since that my penitence comes after all" (l. 304), that is, after his father's deed. But the very process of protecting Henry V's purity by confining the blame to Henry IV suggests its implausibility. Because of the indissoluble union of father and son that derives from their original atonement, Henry V cannot so easily scapegoat his father. The sense of resignation the new king conveys in this moment is an oblique admission that his own royal power as well as his father's may be contaminated. Yet Henry V ultimately turns his anxiety into a joke, seeing the link between his "father's ambition" and "civil wars" as the cause of his "aspect of iron" that frightens Kate (5.2.225–28).

II

Most readers find Henry V's soliloquy in act 4, scene 1, an extraordinarily powerful moment. The crucial questions it poses for interpretation are: what is the place of the soliloquy in the play as a whole? how do we experience the remainder of the play? how are we to understand the king's turning from meditation to battle—"The day, my friends, and all things wait for me" (4.1.309)? One response is to treat the soliloquy in isolation—as a fleeting, inward glimpse that underscores precisely what we do not find elsewhere in the play. J. Dover Wilson, however, [in his edition of the play] has demonstrated the possibility of integrating the soliloquy into the ongoing action, seeing it as a part of a continuous sequence of Henry V's development and growth. In particular, the soliloquy is a spiritual crisis that not only humanizes but tests and strengthens him, enabling him to face the upcoming battle with "the ultimate heroic faith." My own view is that Henry V's heroic faith remains problematic and that Shakespeare does not ask for simple assent to it, but Wilson is right in not splitting the soliloquy off from the rest of the play. There are several dramatic elements in the final section of *Henry*

V that are integrally connected with the emotions emerging in the king's soliloquy.

The encounter with Henry IV's guilt is not simply left behind, but actively suppressed. The emphatic vision of blood brotherhood following Henry V's soliloquy dissolves and evades the burden of paternal sin:

> We would not die in that man's company
> That fears his fellowship to die with us.
>
> . . . .
>
> We few, we happy few, we band of brothers;
> For he to-day that sheds his blood with me
> Shall be my brother.
>
> (4.3.38–39, 60–62)

The quality of elation in his speech can be explained in part by the way its stress on male fellowship takes the pressure off the father–son tension enacted in act 4, scene 1. The "band of brothers" gains its cohesiveness from being selective as well as nonhierarchical: "And gentlemen in England, now a-bed, / Shall think themselves accurs'd they were not here; / And hold their manhoods cheap" (64–66). Ironically, such sacrificial brotherhood has the potential to restore harmony across generations: "This story shall the good man teach his son" (4.3.56).

The particular point in the play that answers to the emotional power of Henry V's story of brotherhood sanctified by bloodshed is the mutual death of York and Suffolk recounted by Exeter in act 4, scene 6. Earlier, Henry V's anticipation of heroic death and fame had included a macabre strain:

> And those that leave their valiant bones in France,
> Dying like men, though buried in your dunghills,
> They shall be fam'd; for there the sun shall greet them,
> And draw their honors reeking up to heaven,
> Leaving their earthly parts to choke your clime,
> The smell whereof shall breed a plague in France.
>
> (4.3.98–103)

Now the grotesque details are sublimated in the fraternal ascension to chronicle heaven:

> Suffolk first died; and York, all haggled over,
> Comes to him, where in gore he lay insteeped,

> And takes him by the beard, kisses the gashes
> That bloodily did yawn upon his face.
> He cries aloud, "Tarry, my cousin Suffolk!
> My soul shall thine keep company to heaven;
> Tarry, sweet soul, for mine, they fly abreast,
> As in this glorious and well-foughten field
> We kept together in our chivalry!"
>
> (4.6.11–19)

At the moment of heroic death, when integration with the rest of one's life is moot, the guard against the normally dreaded effeminacy can be set aside. Expression of affection is compatible with manliness because "honor-owing wounds" (l. 9) are felt to be affirmed by York's embraces.

This ideal of collaborative manhood receives its confirmation when Henry V joins Exeter in indulging in an emotional response to the story:

> EXETER: The pretty and sweet manner of it forc'd
> Those waters from me which I would have stopp'd;
> But I had not so much of man in me,
> And all my mother came into mine eyes
> And gave me up to tears. KING: I blame you not;
> For hearing this, I must perforce compound
> With mistful eyes, or they will issue too.
> But hark, what new alarum is this same?
>
> (4.6.28–35)

Henry V's vicarious participation is sharply curtailed as he is immediately called away to demonstrate once more his toughness. Nonetheless, a moment is long enough to secure the king's approval of this heroic male tenderness. In the company of trusted men, the "mother" can be let out briefly to bear witness to men's quasi-maternal cherishing of one another. The kiss which "espous'd" York to death and to Suffolk and which "seal'd / A testament of noble-ending love" (ll. 25–27) is, in its way, moving; but finally it is unsatisfying because too satisfying.

From our perspective, the witness's allusion to "the pretty and sweet manner of it" (4.6.28) refers not only to the incident but also to his telling of it. This phrase indicates Shakespeare's ability critically to place such an episode of idealized male comradeship. In

Henry V, Shakespeare is not simply victimized by the sentimental dream of self-contained masculine purity; rather, he consciously dramatizes this dream. The narrative frame and style of act 4, scene 6, convey an overly precious, cloying, pseudoarchaic tone that allows Shakespeare to present the chivalric ideal exemplified by the York–Suffolk story as anachronistic convention. The York–Suffolk set piece is a microcosm of the historical as well as psychological escapism implicit in Henry V's heroic impulse.

In the second tetralogy, two historical frames of reference are superimposed: the period 1399–1420, which is the most obvious content of the plays, is implicitly seen from the vantage point of 1595–99, the time of actual composition. As Shakespeare's use of the history play becomes more sophisticated, he shows increasing awareness of the distinction and conflict between medieval and Renaissance cultural modes. In *England in the Late Middle Ages* A. R. Myers sees that time as "a changing world" in which there is a "widening gulf between professed aims and reality":

> Take, for instance, the ideas of chivalry; its feats of heroism in single combat, its crusades and adventures, its code of feudal loyalty and courtly love were appropriate to the feudal order, but by the end of the thirteenth century this had lost its vitality. Yet the militant aristocracy of the late middle ages professed to find in chivalry its guiding principles, and the chroniclers who, like Froissart, wrote to please noble patrons echoes their beliefs. The outward forms of chivalry remained and flourished; tournaments and trappings of chivalry became more splendid, chivalrous courtesy and etiquette became stricter and more complex, orders of knighthood increased in number and pomp. But in human relationships, especially those of rulers, the spirit of chivalry was dying; by the late fifteenth century the crusading impulse, for example, was dead, though kings like Edward IV and Henry VII could still pay lip service to it.

Henry V enacts this tension between the "outward forms" and the "dead spirit" of chivalry. By the time of *Henry V,* Shakespeare has made a fundamental shift of perspective. The pursuit and attainment of honor is no longer considered an exemplary thing in itself but rather as a function of some other context, in particular, the contexts of political skill and conscience. In the new perspective, monolithic commitment to chivalric heroism is seen as anachronistic and reductive (as in the earlier instance of Hotspur).

The other side of this attenuated chivalric coin is the Dauphin, whose mistress is his horse (3.7.42). In the parallel scene to the York–Suffolk apotheosis, the defeated Dauphin draws the appropriate conclusions about his "everlasting shame" (4.5.4). *Henry V*, like *1 Henry VI*, portrays a sharp contrast between the English and the French, a contrast turning on manliness and the lack of it. Talbot in *1 Henry VI* exemplifies the approved image of manhood based on resistance to women and on allegiance to men. Henry V in a more complex way continues this tradition. The English/French contrast in *Henry V* makes possible two separate centers of male comrade-ship—one legitimate and manly, the other its opposite. Herein lies the value of the Dauphin as a travesty of masculinity. His laughable presence diverts and exorcises fears of effeminacy: the English tenderness imaged by York and Suffolk must be virile because the French—epitomized by the Dauphin—are so patently effete.

Yet the Dauphin is paired in rivalry with Henry V. Since one's greatness is measured by the stature of one's rivals, Henry V appears to be mismatched with the Dauphin, who threatens to lower the king to his level (as he cannot be raised to the king's). In their bondedness, rivals mirror each other: the Dauphin casts a bad image on Henry V against which the latter's oratory proves an inadequate defense. Prior to his predictable humiliation, the Dauphin plays a stronger role than his actual weakness would lead us to expect. Like Hotspur (*1H4*, 5.2.69–71), the Dauphin is fooled by Hal's disguise as a wastrel (*H5*, 1.2.250–53). The fact that the Dauphin is an amusingly ineffectual version of Hotspur is part of the dramatic point. The Dauphin forces Henry V to reassert in stronger terms his original strategy of holiday surprise:

> And like bright metal on a sullen ground,
> My reformation, glitt'ring o'er my fault,
> Shall show more goodly and attract more eyes
> Than that which hath no foil to set it off.
> (*1H4*, 1.2.212–15)

> And we understand him well,
> How he comes o'er us with our wilder days,
> Not measuring what use we made of them.

. . . .
> For that I have laid by my majesty
> And plodded like a man for working-days;
> But I will rise there with so full a glory
> That I will dazzle all the eyes of France,
> Yea, strike the Dauphin blind to look on us.
>
> (*H5*, 1.2.266–68, 276–80)

The Dauphin is a "foil" who arouses a depth of anger out of proportion to his provision of a target to satisfy it. The disparity between the Dauphin's taunt with the tennis balls and Henry V's overwrought counterattack (ll. 259–97) embarrasses the king, making it appear that the Dauphin's frivolous gesture has hit a tender nerve. The king can remove his rival's threat only by silencing him, yet no direct encounter parallel to that between Hal and Hotspur in *1 Henry IV* is hazarded. Instead, the Dauphin simply vanishes, his place as son taken over by Henry V.

In his battle rhetoric, the king envisages two images of father–son relations. His heroic appeal to his own men presupposes an ideal harmony:

> On, on, you noblest English,
> Whose blood is fet from fathers of war-proof!
> Fathers that, like so many Alexanders,
> Have in these parts from morn till even fought.
>
> . . . .
> now attest
> That those whom you call'd fathers did beget you.
>
> (3.1.17–20, 22–23)

The obverse, his threatening the French with family destruction, countenances aggression against the father: "Your fathers taken by the silver beards, / And their most reverend heads dash'd to the walls" (3.3.36–37). This double image of the father is embodied specifically in Henry V's contrasting attitudes toward Henry IV and the king of France.

As a father–son pair, the French king and the Dauphin serve the same function as Northumberland and Hotspur by offering a corrupted, negative version of the bond between Henry IV and Hal. The anger, doubt, and criticism that Henry V feels toward his father in the despairing soliloquy of act 4, scene 1, are stifled. But these same feelings can be directed without reservation toward the king of

France, whose enfeebled position invites scorn. At the same time, Henry V can punish his own illicit parricidal impulses by casting the Dauphin in the role of the undependable bad son who deserves to be beaten.

Prompted by the tennis balls, Henry V takes self-righteous pleasure in blaming his attack on the father on the unreliable son's misbehavior: "We will in France, by God's grace, play a set / Shall strike his father's crown into the hazard"; "God before, / We'll chide this Dolphin at his father's door" (1.2.262–63, 307–8). In the final scene, Henry V relishes his control over the French king when he blandly assures Katherine that her father will approve their marriage: "Nay, it will please him well, Kate; it shall please him" (5.2.248–49). Henry V insists on his formal titles as son and heir to the French king (ll. 335–42) partly because it makes legitimate his psychological diplomacy:

> FRANCE. Nor this I have not, brother, so denied,
> But your request shall make me let it pass.
> HENRY. I pray you then, in love and dear alliance,
> Let that one article rank with the rest,
> And thereupon give me your daughter.
> FRANCE. Take her, fair son, and from her blood raise up
> Issue to me.
> (ll. 343–49)

The French king's inevitable yielding establishes a protocol whereby Henry V resolves the contradictory actions of conquering the father and of being accepted harmoniously as his rightful successor. Making his submission complete, the French king calls Henry V not "brother" (l. 343) but "fair son" (l. 348). The father he has ignominiously defeated thus transforms this conquest into a saccharine vision of peace—"and this dear conjunction / Plant neighborhood and Christian-like accord / In their sweet bosoms, that never war advance / His bleeding sword 'twixt England and fair France" (5.2.352–55). How unrealistic this fantasy of unity Henry V elicits, the final chorus soon reminds us.

In the concluding scene the characters try to play a comedy. Burgundy sets the stage by pulling out comic stops reminiscent of the recovery from pastoral disorder in *A Midsummer Night's Dream* (2.1.82–117). Recounting the chaos in nature created by war (*H5*, 5.2.38–62), Burgundy imagines the restoration of the "Dear nurse of art, plenties, and joyful births" that could make "Our fertile France" once again the "best garden of the world" (ll. 35–37). This general pattern of comic denouement is reinforced by conspicuous allusion to the convention equating closure with wedding. The play ends with a performance of epithalamic blessing:

> God, the best of all marriages,
> Combine your hearts in one, your realms in one!
> As man and wife, being two are one in love,
> So be there 'twixt your kingdoms such a spousal,
> That never may ill office, or fell jealousy,
> Which troubles oft the bed of blessed marriage.
>
> (ll. 359–64)

Yet we are prevented from taking full comic satisfaction in this marital hopefulness not only because the chorus throws cold water on the political harmony it envisions but also because the actual courtship we have witnessed is not an unqualified success.

Henry V applies himself to wooing with a gusto appropriate to comic decorum. His inability "to mince it in love" (5.2.126) and his plain speaking are often taken as evidence of an engaging bluntness. Yet the language barrier creates difficulty as well as humor. Kate's role as unresponsive straw woman blocks the quick conclusion Harry seeks— "Give me your answer, i' faith, do, and so clap hands and a bargain" (ll. 129–30). Though he maintains an unflappable, upbeat tone, his bravado becomes repetitious, his "downright oaths" (l. 144) feeling less and less funny and enjoyable. He seems reduced to a "fellow of infinite tongue" (l. 156), who keeps "wearing out his suit" (ll. 128–29). As elsewhere in the play, Henry V is here forced to talk too much, endlessly to justify himself.

The emphatic soldier identity (5.2.99, 149, 166) that the king brings to the courtship undermines as much as it promotes a comic spirit. He looks beyond wooing to the son this marriage can produce to carry on Christian military exploits, thereby turning Kate into "a good soldier-breeder" (l. 206). The tension between political opportunity and love has been present from the outset. The king's marriage does not depend on the outcome of the private wooing scene since, as he announces, his power to enforce his desires is guaranteed in advance: "She is our capital demand, compris'd / Within the fore-rank of our articles" (l. 96–97). This externally imposed conclusion casts some doubt on the status of Henry V's love by raising the possibility that mechanical appropriation substitutes for, rather than coincides with, genuine feeling. But the king's love is also subject to question on internal grounds.

The ultimate reason for the deep awkwardness beneath the comic surface in the courtship scene comes from the way Henry V's "speaking plain soldier" (5.2.149) causes him to portray sexuality as a form of military aggression and conquest. Phrases like "I love thee cruelly" and "I get thee with scambling" (ll. 202–3, 204–5) contain ironies the king cannot control. The exuberant mixing of love and war comes naturally to Henry V:

> If I could win a lady at leap-frog, or by vaulting into my saddle with my armor on my back, under the correction of bragging be it spoken, I should quickly leap into a wife. Or if I might buffet for my love, or bound my horse for her favors, I could lay on like a butcher, and sit like a jack-an-apes, never off.
>
> (ll. 136–42)

The issue here is not bragging but the metaphorical equation of woman with horse, an equation the Dauphin has taught us: "O then belike she was old and gentle, and you rode like a kern of Ireland, your French hose off, and in your straight strossers (3.7.52–54). Henry V's wooing in the final scene implicitly culminates his rivalry with the Dauphin, which had a sexual current from the start in the challenge presented by the tennis balls. One does not need the conflict between the clowns—"Pistol's cock is up" (2.1.52)—to alert us to the phallic implication of the king's conversion of "balls to gunstones" (1.2.282). The sexual reference of "the Paris balls" is confirmed by the threat of war that puns on lover: "He'll make your Paris Louvre shake for it, / Were it the mistress court of mighty Europe" (2.4.131–33).

The French anticipate their defeat in sexual terms:

> Our madams mock at us, and plainly say
> Our mettle is bred out, and they will give
> Their bodies to the lust of English youth
> To new-store France with bastard warriors.
> (3.5.28–31)

> Let him go hence, and with his cap in hand
> Like a base pander hold the chamber-door

> Whilst by a slave, no gentler than my dog,
> His fairest daughter is contaminated.
>
> (4.5.13–16)

Henry V's wartime oratory had promised no less (3.3.11–14, 20–21, 33–35), while his peacetime approach holds this threat in abeyance as in the elaborate banter likening Katherine to French cities "all girdled with maiden walls that war hath never ent'red" (5.2.321–23). The king's coarseness in the wooing scene loses much of its comic appeal because it participates in the troubled sexuality displayed throughout the play. The "frankness" of Henry V's "mirth" (l. 291) is finally a sexual humor that can be shared only by men, as his turning to Burgundy for support suggests: "Yet they do wink and yield, as love is blind and enforces" (ll. 300–301). The enmity between French and English men is in part resolved because they can unite in erotic humor at Katherine's expense.

The second tetralogy of English history plays avoids the threat to male rule that formidable women present in the first tetralogy by restricting women to the periphery. In *Richard II,* the Duchess of Gloucester and Richard's queen can complain or lament but cannot genuinely threaten. The Duchess of York is neutralized by being treated as a source of comedy. Richard, who sees himself in relation to his kingdom as a "mother with her child" (3.2.8), is himself eliminated in favor of the apparently more promising masculinity of Bolingbroke. The women in the *Henry IV* plays have an even more marginal existence. The spirited wit and brusque affection in Hotspur's relationship with Kate are relatively insignificant given his clear statement of priorities:

> This is no world
> To play with mammets and to tilt with lips.
> We must have bloody noses and crack'd crowns,
> And pass them current too. God's me, my horse!
>
> (*1H4,* 2.3.91–94)

The emphasis on chivalric warfare rather than chivalric love applies even more so to Hal, who participates in the convention of masculine purity automatically because he is not compromised by any connections to a woman. For the purposes of the second tetralogy, Hal is not "of woman born." Coppélia Kahn convincingly argues that Hal's association with Falstaff "represents the wish to bypass women." In this regard, the similarity between Falstaff and the wifeless Henry IV makes Hal's transition from one to the other relatively easy. Hal's reunion with his father continues to fulfill the need to bypass women; the rejection of Falstaff and the reconciliation with Henry IV in no way disrupts Hal-Henry V's commitment to male bonding.

The ending of *Henry V* proposes to round out the king's character by providing him with a woman, but this proposal cannot be enacted because his character is too entrenched in a narrow masculinity. All emotional depth is concentrated in male relations. Henry V's attempt to conclude a relationship with Katherine in the final scene is the exception that proves the general rule. The residual awkwardness of the king's wooing of Kate cannot be attributed simply to inexperience with women, nor can it be joked away because there is a more specific obstacle: the counterpull of male bonding, whose strength has been affirmed by the consummation allowed to York and Suffolk. When we compare the "testament of noble-ending love" (4.6.27) offered by York and Suffolk with the king's courtship of Katherine, the two love scenes cannot compete; the power of the earlier instance overshadows the final scene, which seems unfulfilled by comparison. The entire second tetralogy stands behind a military definition of masculinity that cannot be overturned by a last-minute ending.

III

The usual way to make the transition from *Henry V* to *Hamlet* is to link Henry V with Fortinbras. This linkage expresses the view that Henry V is reduced to the political function that he performs so efficiently. A much richer and more accurate way to make the connection is to place Henry V directly in the line that leads to Hamlet. Both young men are poised between two father figures. Each has little or no difficulty in distinguishing and rejecting the false, usurping father. Though he makes use of Falstaff for strategic purposes, Hal is clear from the beginning about his ability to banish him. Claudius, like Falstaff, is a Lord of Misrule who is to be rejected as a politically subversive abuser of holiday festivity. While waiting for the ghost's appearance, Hamlet bitterly criticizes Claudius's drinking as an inappropriate "observance" of "custom" (1.4.16, 15). In both instances it is paradoxically the relationship with the rightful father that the sons find impossible to resolve.

For Hal and Hamlet, it is a problem to experience the declaration that invigorates Orlando: "The spirit of my father grows strong in me." Orlando, who is not forced to deal with the original father, easily secures a benevolent substitute in Duke Senior. For Hal and Hamlet, however, identity is formed and given permanent shape in a decisive encounter with the father. Hal's role is thrust upon him when, at the end of *2 Henry IV,* the dying king not only bequeaths his power but also specifies how his son is to use the kingship. Similarly, the ghost defines Hamlet's destiny. The highly charged confrontation scene is characterized by a mixture of intimacy and distance, by the father's melodramatic anger as well as his melodramatic love. The father urgently challenges and claims the son's love, and this urgency is complicated by the father's insistence on his own deficiencies, which the son is called upon to remedy. Like Cordelia, Henry V and Hamlet "go about their father's business" as well as their own. Ultimately, the paternal injunction is a painful burden for Henry V as well as for Hamlet. Like Cordelia, they become "sacrifices" to their father's idealized visions of vindication and redemption. But, unlike Cordelia, the two men are not silent about their fate.

A sharp contrast between Henry V as a man of action and Hamlet as a man of thought is misleading because both are primarily men of long speeches. In each case, the long speech symbolizes a continual search for a justifiable identity. The urgency of self-definition is intensified by a conscience based on atonement with the father. In both *Henry V* and *Hamlet,* the pressure of the father's demands is manifested in the son's self-conscious acting. Like Hamlet, Hal has put on an antic disposition, which then becomes a lasting problem because the act cannot be discontinued at will. Hal as Henry V is a player king who unsuccessfully attempts to stage situations that will give his identity complete credibility.

The continuity between *Henry V* and *Hamlet* appears in other ways as well. The disturbed relationship between men and women exemplified in the Henry V–Katherine courtship anticipates the more overt instance of Hamlet and Ophelia. Henry V's image of male bonding between brothers as an alternative to the problematic tension of father–son relations—an image crystallized in the York–Suffolk scene—connects with Hamlet's reliance on the faithful comrade Horatio, to whom in the final scene he entrusts his story. Both Henry V and Hamlet are poised between the two incompatible options of male and heterosexual ties. In both cases, forms of male bonding take precedence at the expense of relations with women. *Hamlet* more directly confronts alienation from women, but the ending of *Henry V,* in raising yet not fulfilling festive marital expectations, reveals the problem. In thus helping to prepare the way for *Hamlet's* treatment of male–male and male–female relations, *Henry V* should be viewed not as an artistic backwater in Shakespeare's development but as part of the mainstream. To acknowledge the central position of *Henry V* as the link between the second tetralogy and *Hamlet,* we must see that the play cuts deeper than Henry V's military success and gives dramatic weight to his psychological complexity.

Henry V dramatizes the gap between the received story and the identity that actually emerges. Henry V tries rhetorically to close the gap between expectations and actuality; his failure to do so means that identity becomes an open question, as happens more spectacularly in the tragedies. The relentless quality of Henry V's language comes from the stressfulness of this irreducible gap. It is as though he keeps redoing the image he projects in the speeches in an effort to make it come out right. But validation of identity through chronicle eludes him because his identity is too heterogeneous to fit the epic image. Hence, Henry V is placed in a tragic condition despite the lack of a catastrophic tragic denouement. It is left to the final Chorus, from its perspective outside the dramatic action, to strike a tragic note.

Chronology

1564	William Shakespeare born at Stratford-on-Avon to John Shakespeare, a butcher, and Mary Arden. He is baptized on April 26.
1582	Marries Anne Hathaway in November.
1583	Daughter Susanna born, baptized on May 26.
1585	Twins Hamnet and Judith born, baptized on February 2.
1588–90	Sometime during these years, Shakespeare goes to London, without family. First plays performed in London.
1590–92	*The Comedy of Errors,* the three parts of *Henry VI.*
1593–94	Publication of *Venus and Adonis* and *The Rape of Lucrece,* both dedicated to the Earl of Southampton. Shakespeare becomes a sharer in the Lord Chamberlain's company of actors. *The Taming of the Shrew, The Two Gentlemen of Verona, Richard III, Titus Andronicus.*
1595–97	*Romeo and Juliet, Richard II, King John, A Midsummer Night's Dream, Love's Labor's Lost.*
1596	Son Hamnet dies. Grant of arms to Shakespeare's father.
1597	*The Merchant of Venice, Henry IV, Part 1.* Purchases New Place in Stratford.
1598–1600	*Henry IV, Part 2, As You Like It, Much Ado about Nothing, Twelfth Night, The Merry Wives of Windsor, Henry V,* and *Julius Caesar.* Moves his company to the new Globe Theatre.
1601	*Hamlet.* Shakespeare's father dies, buried on September 8.

1601–2	*Troilus and Cressida.*
1603	Death of Queen Elizabeth; James VI of Scotland becomes James I of England; Shakespeare's company becomes the King's Men.
1603–4	*All's Well That Ends Well, Measure for Measure, Othello.*
1605–6	*King Lear, Macbeth.*
1607	Marriage of daughter Susanna on June 5.
1607–8	*Timon of Athens, Antony and Cleopatra, Pericles, Coriolanus.*
1608	Shakespeare's mother dies, buried on September 9.
1609	*Cymbeline,* publication of sonnets. Shakespeare's company purchases Blackfriars Theatre.
1610–11	*The Winter's Tale, The Tempest.* Shakespeare retires to Stratford.
1612–13	*Henry VIII, The Two Noble Kinsmen.*
1616	Marriage of daughter Judith on February 10. Shakespeare dies at Stratford on April 23.
1623	Publication of the Folio edition of Shakespeare's plays.

Contributors

HAROLD BLOOM, Sterling Professor of the Humanities at Yale University, is the author of *The Anxiety of Influence, Poetry and Repression,* and many other volumes of literary criticism. His forthcoming study, *Freud: Transference and Authority,* attempts a full-scale reading of all of Freud's major writings. A MacArthur Prize Fellow, he is general editor of five series of literary criticism published by Chelsea House. During 1987–88, he served as Charles Eliot Norton Professor of Poetry at Harvard University.

ANNE BARTON is Professor of English at Cambridge University. She is the author of *Shakespeare and the Idea of the Play* and *Ben Jonson, Dramatist.*

JAMES L. CALDERWOOD is Associate Dean of Humanities at the University of California at Irvine. He is the author of *Metadrama in Shakespeare's Henriad.*

NORMAN RABKIN, Professor of English at the University of California at Berkeley, is the author of *Shakespeare and the Common Understanding* and *Shakespeare and the Problem of Meaning.*

DAVID QUINT is Associate Professor of Comparative Literature at Princeton University. He is the author of *Origin and Originality in Renaissance Literature: Versions of the Source* and the translator of *The Stanze of Angelo Poliziano.*

JAMES R. SIEMON, Assistant Professor of English at Boston University, is the author of *Shakespearean Iconoclasm.*

JONATHAN DOLLIMORE, Lecturer in English at the University of Sussex, is the author of *Radical Tragedy* and the co-editor of *Political Shakespeare: New Essays in Cultural Materialism.*

ALAN SINFIELD, Reader in English at the University of Sussex, is the author of books on Renaissance and Victorian literature and is the co-editor of *Political Shakespeare: New Essays in Cultural Materialism.*

PETER ERICKSON teaches English at Wesleyan University. He is the author of *Patriarchal Structures in Shakespeare's Drama.*

Bibliography

Altieri, Joanne. "Romance in *Henry V.*" *Studies in English Literature 1500–1900* 21, no. 2 (1981): 223–40.

Babula, William. "Whatever Happened to Prince Hal? An Essay on *Henry V.*" *Shakespeare Survey* 30 (1977): 47–59.

Battenhouse, Roy. "*Henry V* as Heroic Comedy." In *Essays on Shakespeare and Elizabethan Drama,* edited by Richard Hosley. Columbia: University of Missouri Press, 1962.

Bergeron, David M. *Pageantry in the Shakespearean Theater.* Athens: University of Georgia Press, 1985.

Berry, Edward I. " 'True Things and Mock'ries': Epic and History in *Henry V.*" *Journal of English and Germanic Philology* 78 (1979): 1–16.

Brennan, Anthony S. "That Within Which Passes Show: The Function of the Chorus in *Henry V.*" *Philological Quarterly* 58 (1979): 40–52.

Brown, William J. "*Henry V* and *Tamburlaine:* The Structural and Thematic Relationship." *Iowa State Journal of Research* 57, no. 2 (1982): 113–22.

Bullough, Geoffrey, ed. *Narrative and Dramatic Sources of Shakespeare.* London: Routledge & Kegan Paul, 1962.

Burckhardt, Sigurd. *Shakespearean Meanings.* Princeton: Princeton University Press, 1968.

Campbell, Lily B. *Shakespeare's "Histories": Mirrors of Elizabethan Policy.* San Marino, Calif.: Huntington Library, 1978.

Collins, David. "On Re-Interpreting *Henry V.*" *Upstart Crow* 4 (Fall 1982): 18–34.

Coursen, H. R. *The Leasing Out of England.* Washington, D.C.: University Press of America, 1982.

Danson, Lawrence. "*Henry V:* King, Chorus, and Critics." *Shakespeare Quarterly* 34 (1983): 27–43.

Davison, Peter. Henry V *in the Context of the Popular Dramatic Tradition.* Winchester: King Alfred's College, 1981.

Dean, Paul. "Chronicle and Romance Modes in *Henry V.*" *Shakespeare Quarterly* 32 (1981): 18–27.

Dollimore, Jonathan, and Alan Sinfield, eds. *Political Shakespeare: New Essays in Cultural Materialism.* Manchester: Manchester University Press, 1985.

Egan, Robert. "A Muse of Fire: *Henry V* in the Light of *Tamburlaine.*" *Modern Language Quarterly* 29 (1968): 15–28.

Ellis-Fermor, Una. "Shakespeare's Political Plays." In *The Frontiers of Drama*. London: Methuen, 1945.

Erickson, Peter B. " 'The Fault / My Father's Made': The Anxious Pursuit of Heroic Fame in Shakespeare's *Henry V.*" *Modern Language Studies* 10, no. 1 (1979–80): 10–25.

Fleissner, R. F. "Putting Falstaff to Rest: 'Tabulating' the Facts." *Shakespeare Survey* 16 (1983): 57–74.

Goddard, Harold C. *The Meaning of Shakespeare*. Chicago: University of Chicago Press, 1951.

Goldman, Michael. *Shakespeare and the Energies of Drama*. Princeton: Princeton University Press, 1972.

Granville-Barker, Harley. *More Prefaces to Shakespeare*. Princeton: Princeton University Press, 1974.

Grennan, Eamon. " 'This Story Shall the Good Man Teach His Son': *Henry V* and the Art of History." *Papers in Language and Literature* 15 (1979): 370–82.

Gurr, Andrew. "*Henry V* and the Bee's Commonwealth." *Shakespeare Survey* 30 (1977): 61–72.

Hawkins, Sherman H. "Virtue and Kingship in Shakespeare's *Henry IV.*" *English Literary Renaissance* 5 (1975): 313–43.

Holderness, Graham. "Agincourt 1944: Readings in the Shakespearean Myth." *Literature and History* 10, no. 1 (1984): 24–45.

———. *Shakespeare's History*. Dublin: Gill & Macmillan, 1985.

Hotson, Leslie. *Shakespeare's Sonnets Dated, and Other Essays*. London: R. Hart-Davis, 1949.

Jenkins, Harold. "Shakespeare's History Plays: 1900–1951." *Shakespeare Survey* 6 (1953): 1–15.

Jones, G. P. "*Henry V*: The Chorus and the Audience." *Shakespeare Survey* 31 (1978): 93–104.

Kahn, Coppélia. *Man's Estate: Masculine Identity in Shakespeare*. Berkeley: University of California Press, 1981.

Kernan, Alvin B. "The Henriad: Shakespeare's Major History Plays." In *Modern Shakespearean Criticism: Essays on Style, Dramaturgy and the Major Plays*, edited by Alvin Kernan, 245–75. New York: Harcourt, Brace, 1970.

Knights, L. C. *Shakespeare's Politics: With Some Reflections upon the Nature of Tradition*. London: Oxford University Press, 1958.

Kott, Jan. *Shakespeare Our Contemporary*. 2d ed. London: Methuen, 1967.

Levin, Richard. "Hazlitt on *Henry V*, and the Appropriation of Shakespeare." *Shakespeare Quarterly* 35 (1984): 134–41.

MacDonald, Gina, and Andrew MacDonald. "*Henry V*: A Shakespearean Definition of Politic Reign." *Studies in the Humanities* 9, no. 2 (1982): 32–39.

Ornstein, Robert. *A Kingdom for a Stage: The Achievement of Shakespeare's History Plays*. Cambridge: Harvard University Press, 1972.

Palmer, John L. *Political Characters in Shakespeare*. London: Macmillan, 1945.

Platt, Michael. "Falstaff in the Valley of the Shadow of Death." *Interpretation: Journal of Political Philosophy* 8, no. 1 (1979): 5–29.

Prior, Moody. *The Drama of Power: Studies in Shakespeare's History Plays*. Evanston, Ill.: Northwestern University Press, 1973.

Rabkin, Norman. *Shakespeare and the Common Understanding.* New York: The Free Press, 1967.

Richardson, W. M. "The Brave New World of Shakespeare's *Henry V* Revisited." *Allegorica* 6, no. 2 (1981): 149–54.

Rossiter, A. P. "Ambivalence—The Dialectic of the Histories." In *Angel with Horns.* New York: Theatre Art Books, 1961.

Saccio, Peter. *Shakespeare's English Kings.* London: Oxford University Press, 1977.

Salomon, Brownell. "Thematic Contraries and the Dramaturgy of *Henry V.*" *Shakespeare Quarterly* 31 (1980): 343–56.

Smith, Gordon Ross. "Shakespeare's *Henry V:* Another Part of the Critical Forest." *Journal of the History of Ideas* 37 (1976): 3–26.

Tillyard, E. M. W. *The Elizabethan World Picture.* Harmondsworth: Penguin, 1960.

———. *Shakespeare's History Plays.* Harmondsworth: Penguin, 1962.

Traversi, D. A. *Shakespeare: From Richard II to Henry V.* Stanford: Stanford University Press, 1957.

Van den Berg, Kent T. *Playhouse and Cosmos: Shakespearean Theater as Metaphor.* Newark: University of Delaware Press, 1984.

Webber, Joan. "The Renewal of the King's Symbolic Role: From *Richard II* to *Henry V.*" *Texas Studies in Literature and Language* 4 (1963): 530–38.

Wentersdorf, Karl P. "The Conspiracy of Silence in *Henry V.*" *Shakespeare Quarterly* 27 (1976): 264–87.

Wilson, J. Dover. *The Fortunes of Falstaff.* Cambridge: Cambridge University Press, 1943.

Acknowledgments

"The King Disguised: The Two Bodies of Henry V" (originally entitled "The King Disguised: Shakespeare's *Henry V* and the Comical History") by Anne Barton from *The Triple Bond: Plays, Mainly Shakespearean, in Performance,* edited by Joseph G. Price, © 1975 by Pennsylvania State University. Reprinted by permission of the Pennsylvania State University Press.

"*Henry V:* English, Rhetoric, Theater" by James L. Calderwood from *Metadrama in Shakespeare's Henriad:* Richard II *to* Henry V by James L. Calderwood, © 1979 by the Regents of the University of California. Reprinted by permission of the University of California Press.

"Either/Or: Responding to *Henry V*" by Norman Rabkin from *Shakespeare and the Problem of Meaning* by Norman Rabkin, © 1981 by the University of Chicago. Reprinted by permission of the author and the University of Chicago Press.

" 'Alexander the Pig': Shakespeare on History and Poetry" by David Quint from *boundary 2* 10, no. 3 (Spring 1982), © 1982 by *boundary 2.* Reprinted by permission.

"The 'Image Bound': Icon and Iconoclasm in *Henry V*" (originally entitled "The 'Image Bound': Icon and Iconoclasm in *Lucrece* and *Henry V*") by James R. Siemon from *Shakespearean Iconoclasm* by James R. Siemon, © 1985 by the Regents of the University of California. Reprinted by permission of the University of California Press.

"History and Ideology: The Instance of *Henry V*" by Jonathan Dollimore and Alan Sinfield from *Alternative Shakespeares,* edited by John Drakakis, © 1985 by Jonathan Dollimore and Alan Sinfield. Reprinted by permission.

"Fathers, Sons, and Brothers in *Henry V*" by Peter Erickson from *Patriarchal Structures in Shakespeare's Drama* by Peter Erickson, © 1985 by the Regents of the University of California. Reprinted by permission of the University of California Press.

Index